IMAGES
of America

THE SAN JOSE
POLICE DEPARTMENT

Various patches worn by the San Jose Police Department are pictured here. (Courtesy of the San Jose Police Historical Society.)

ON THE COVER: Chief John N. Black (front passenger), officer James Prindiville (driver), officer Luis O. Pfau (rear left), and officer Peter Benjamine (rear right) are seated in a 1907 Rambler Sedan on Market Street, facing south (note the dome for St. Joseph's in the background). The building to the right is San Jose City Hall, where the chief of police's office is located in the back corner on the bottom floor. This very formal photograph of the officers and the Rambler has been publicized as showing San Jose's first police car, but in actuality, this was just an opportunity for the officers to take a novelty photograph while seated inside of the vehicle when it was brought to city hall. (Courtesy of the San Jose Police Historical Society.)

IMAGES
of America

THE SAN JOSE
POLICE DEPARTMENT

John Carr Jr. and Jarrod J. Nunes

ARCADIA
PUBLISHING

Published by Arcadia Publishing
Charleston, South Carolina

Library of Congress Control Number: 2013946474

For all general information, please contact Arcadia Publishing:
Telephone 843-853-2070
Fax 843-853-0044
E-mail sales@arcadiapublishing.com
For customer service and orders:
Toll-Free 1-888-313-2665

Visit us on the Internet at www.arcadiapublishing.com

CONTENTS

ACKNOWLEDGMENTS

We would like to thank and recognize all the men and women who have put on the San Jose Police uniform and worn it with pride and honor over the last 163 years of our existence. We would especially like to honor the 11 San Jose police officers who have paid the ultimate sacrifice and lost their lives in the line of duty. We undertook this project to preserve the history of this great police department by telling the stories and history that would otherwise be forgotten. A special thank-you to all those who helped see our project through, providing photographs, factual information, and most importantly, stories. Those that have passed through these streets have laid the foundation for the next generation to build upon.

Special thanks go to the Martin Luther King Jr. Library California Room, History San Jose, the San Jose Police Benevolent Association, the San Jose Police Officers Association, San Jose police chief Larry Esquivel, the Honorable Judge Dolores Carr (retired) for proofreading the drafts, Lt. Eduardo Pedriera, Lt. Bob Moir (retired), Lt. John Carr Sr. (retired), Lt. Joe Nunes (retired), Lt. Rick Botar (retired), Sgt. Aubrey Parrot (retired), officer Bill Mattos (retired), officer Leroy Pyle (retired), officer Pete Guerin (retired), officer William Rendler (retired), officer John Shuman (retired), officer Terry "Greek" Moudakas, officer Trevor Condon, officer Greg Grothaus, Kathy Smith (for providing information on Alviso Police Department), Shannon Carr, Lew Smith, and especially Lon Miner for all his patience and help scanning, organizing, and cleaning old photographs. We would like to express our sincere thanks to our family and friends, who played an important role in the publication of this book, especially in giving us the support and motivation to complete it.

Unless otherwise noted, all images appear courtesy of the San Jose Police Historical Society collection. All author royalties from the sales of this book will go to the San Jose Police Historical Society (www.SanJosePoliceHistoricalSociety.com).

INTRODUCTION

San Jose is located approximately 40 miles south of San Francisco, just at the edge of San Francisco Bay. Spread out over 177 square miles and with a population over just over one million people, San Jose has continued to grow at a steady pace since its establishment in 1777. San Jose became world renowned in the 1800s and 1900s as the "Valley of the Heart's Delight," providing a large portion of the world's supply of agriculture and canning. This development took a different direction in the 1950s when a small company called International Business Machines (IBM) opened and developed several campuses in San Jose. The new industry took root and spread quickly throughout the area, with San Jose in the lead as the "capital of Silicon Valley."

In the early days, San Jose was a major agricultural farming community, with acres of fruit trees of every type. Throughout the 1800s, it became a very rough place, with gambling, prostitution, and alcohol-related crimes prevalent. The surrounding country was very sparsely populated, which made it difficult to catch criminals. Often, people took the law into their own hands through lynching and vigilantism.

In 1849, after the Mexican-American War and California's entry to the United States, a formalized municipal government—with a mayor and seven councilmen—was created. On September 24, 1849, the city council appointed 12 men the first officers in the San Jose Police Department. In November 1849, James Frazier Reed (a survivor of the ill-fated Donner-Reed Party) was appointed chief of police.

In order to become an officer candidate, one had to have a petition signed by a certain number of residents within his ward (a geographic section of town). The city council would then ratify the officer's appointment. With the approval of the right political powers, a job could be obtained. Some officers had prior experience in their former homelands, but most were from a farming background. Education levels varied as well, but most officers were literate. Very few actually graduated high school. Pay was $75 per month, and the chief earned $125.

At the turn of the century, the new horseless carriage began to wreak havoc on both man and livery. This led to the creation of a traffic-enforcement unit (which has served without interruption since 1903). Modern advances, such as long-distance passenger-train service, telephones, and telegraph service, enabled more citizens to contact the police department and ensured a more rapid response. Officers without a personal motorcycle or vehicle to use were assigned to posts at specific corners of downtown to monitor everything from traffic to vagrancy. Once a formal police department was firmly established, San Jose quickly developed a reputation for being on the forefront of innovation. The ranks grew steadily, and by 1919, there were 26 sworn officers.

Prior to 1930, there was no organized police training for new officers. New patrolmen were placed on a walking beat and expected to gain on-the-job experience and use common sense. In 1930, a police school was started at San Jose State College. It was a two-year program for applicants interested in law enforcement and in-service police personnel. The school fell under the auspices of the Department of Social Science and was known as the Police Administration Course. In 1935, the school was made a separate department of the college, and in 1938, it awarded its first bachelor of arts degree.

In 1940, the department consisted of a chief of police, two captains, and approximately 100 patrolmen. This was a time of great expansion and growth in the San Jose community. On December 7, 1941, the United States was plunged into World War II with the surprise attack on Pearl Harbor. On December 8, 1941, Chief John Black called for the formation of a civilian emergency police unit that would be a part of the police department. In 1942, funds were diverted to allow an officer to do undercover work with the FBI to seek out people dealing in black-market war equipment, materials, and gas coupons. Between 1941 and 1945, San Jose was swept up in the rapid industrial and military-related growth, an expanding agricultural base, and a steadily increasing population. Special instruction and training about espionage were provided by the FBI, inspired by fears for California's numerous ports and shipyards.

In September 1944, the department began its first formalized in-house training program. This was meant to teach policing techniques learned from the new police schools to officers who were already working. In order to become more open to the public, the department published the first police manual for officers, listing the chain of command, structure of the organization, functions of each of the units within the department, and the purpose of their assignments.

In April 1947, Capt. Ray Blackmore was appointed chief of police, a position he held until 1971, making his the longest tenure of any San Jose police chief. Chief Blackmore's first task was to reorganize the department. The complaint desk became a 24-hour operation and had an assigned desk sergeant. New three-way radios were installed in the cars, which allowed communication from car to car as well as from car to headquarters. In 1947, the first Teletype system was installed in the department; it was tied into a statewide police network. In 1948, as a response to an increase in juvenile delinquency created by both wartime conditions and absent parents, the department established a baseball program with the assistance of the schoolboy patrol program, a predecessor of the current Police Activities League (PAL).

In 1955, the first vice unit was formed to handle prostitution and narcotics sales, use, and possession. Beginning in 1956, officers booked prisoners in the new county jail on Hedding Street instead of the jail at the old police station on Market Street. In 1958, the city and county jails were combined. Prior to 1956, the traffic and patrol divisions had been two separate divisions. That year, they were combined into the uniformed division in order to better maintain supervision and communication.

Several years later, as the city grew at an even faster pace, the police communications and fire communications merged with other city services into the communications department. A new communications center was constructed on the corner of Mission and San Pedro Streets to house the new, state-of-the-art communications equipment.

Officers in 1960 continued handling their duties on foot patrol, as they had for the past 80 years. Because of annexation and sprawl, officers were then patrolling over 74 square miles, the majority of which was farmland.

With the turmoil and social changes of the late 1960s and early 1970s, the department recognized that a special unit would be needed to deal with crime in a new way. Capt. Bill Brown was tapped to form a new specialized unit that would consist of highly motivated, top-notch officers to proactively arrest criminals rather than respond to calls for service. This unit was first called "H-Cars" and, in 1973, was renamed Mobile Emergency Response Group and Equipment, or MERGE.

Great changes came to the department in 1976 with the appointment of Chief Joseph McNamara, the first outsider named to the position. McNamara immediately implemented a transfer policy to move personnel in and out of specialized assignments. This not only allowed individual officers to gather experience in different areas, it also brought together the patrol officers and detectives. Thanks to his leadership, San Jose's became one of the most respected police departments in the nation.

The 1980s brought a new style of policing called "community policing." This style returned officers to working as they had done a century earlier—getting to know the people and the problems in their beats so that they could better address them. The 1990s saw the rebirth of San Jose as the leader in technology in Silicon Valley.

From the early agricultural community to today's big city, San Jose Police Department has been serving its residents with honor and integrity. Highly trained and skilled officers continue to keep the traditions and service standards alive that will serve residents well into the next century.

One

THE EARLY YEARS
1700s–1890s

Prior to the 1770s, the area 40 miles south of San Francisco was inhabited by a peaceful tribe of Ohlone Indians. In 1775, Spain made plans to colonize this area with civilians. An expedition rode up from what is now Southern California and established a pueblo on November 29, 1777. Nine Spanish soldiers lived among the settlers to keep the peace and provide protection, thus becoming the area's first law enforcement officers. San Jose was governed by a *comisionado* who held the rank of corporal or sergeant and whose duty was to enforce all civil and military laws.

The Mexican-American War occurred between 1846 and 1848. San Jose was captured without bloodshed by American forces (led by Capt. James Fallon) in 1846. The United States appointed an alcalde (a combination of mayor, chief justice, and chief of police) as well as two *regidores* (a combination of police officers and city councilmen) to be in charge. One regidor worked the night watch, while another regidor and the alcalde worked during the day. By the end of 1846, there were between six and seven appointed regidores and one alcalde. After the war ended in 1848, California was annexed to the United States.

In November 1848, the council appointed San Jose's first paid law enforcement officer. As first constable, William O'Conner earned $100 per month in gold. The following year, R.C. Keyes was appointed sheriff, and 13 men were drafted to fill part-time positions as town police. Harry Bee was given the duties of *aguazil*, or marshal, and James Frazier Reed became chief of police.

The 1890s were a time of growth and modernization in San Jose. As the population grew, so did the police department. In 1832, San Jose had 10 officers and 2 captains. By 1900, there were 25 officers working the newly established eight-hour shift. In 1897, a board of commissioners was created and empowered to prescribe salary, qualifications, rank, uniforms, and badges of the officers and employees of the police and fire departments. They were also tasked with managing the rules and regulations for the governance and discipline of the departments, as well as prescribing discipline handed down. This body established new, strong standards of police conduct that would influence other law enforcement agencies nationwide.

This is one of the earliest known images of a San Jose police officer and is believed to be from the early to mid-1870s. During this era, officers wore only a badge with a number. It was during this time that the San Jose Police Department was trying to formalize to a standard uniform. Twenty years later, the city council passed a resolution that "uniforms like those of San Francisco will be worn by all members of the regular force. A star on their left breast with the inscription San Jose Police which has an engraved number shall be worn" (San Jose City Charter, Article X, Section 15, 1896).

From left to right, officer P. Mullally, Capt. J.A. Monroe, Chief of Police James A. Kidward, and patrol driver John Humburg stand behind the counter at the police department inside the city hall basement around 1896. Above the officers hang portraits of Chief Kidward (left) and Capt. Thomas Vance (right). Also in 1896, call boxes were installed in the downtown area to allow for citizens to call the police for services. Note the chief's office hours posted on the sign above the gate.

The San Jose Police Department is pictured here between 1884 and 1885 outside of city hall at 35 North Market Street. All wear badges over their left breast to identify themselves as law enforcement officers. From left to right are (first row) Capt. Thomas Vance, Chief William "Billy" Brown, and Capt. J.H. Adams Sr.; (second row) Officer Bardes, William G. Jones, Matt Coschina, E.A. McClintock, Mayor Campbell Settle, August F. Allen, Richard Stewart, John Horn, and unidentified.

This photograph was taken across the street from city hall. Here, the chief is wearing his badge on his left breast. Chief Brown's badge, pictured on the right, was handmade and engraved by a local jeweler in fine silver. Regular patrol officers' badges at this time were made of tin or nickel, stamped "Police Officer," and individually numbered. Many officers had badges presented to them by grateful community groups or citizens that were more elaborate and ornate.

This is the department in 1895. Pictured at center is Chief James A. Kidward. The three directly to the right of the chief are, from top to bottom, George E. Pickering, A.J. Monroe, and E. Evans, and the three to the left are, from top to bottom, William E. Bateman, R.A. Anderson, and D. Campbell. In the outer circle are, clockwise from above center, E.C. Gould, James P. Prindiville, Charles Shannon, Jim Monahan, J.F. Haley, J. Humburg, V. Bacue, Capt. Thomas Vance, O.H. Pfau, John Horn, Theodore Hughes, C.J. Notting, A.F. Allen, and A.E. McClintock. (Note that only officer John Horn is pictured in his uniform.)

The San Jose City Hall and Police Department was located at 35 North Market Street in 1854. At this time, officers were recruited by the alcalde, or town marshal, to perform police functions. There was no training for the officers; the ability to fire a bullet on target was considered sufficient.

This photograph of old city hall was taken in the late 1880s just after the building's completion. It was constructed in 1887 along Market Street, just north of San Carlos Street. This building was used until 1958, at which time a new city hall was constructed at First and Mission Streets. The police department was housed on the lower levels and basement with an underground driveway passing through the middle. The upper levels housed the city government and service offices.

Officer Jim Reed (on horseback) leads a parade north on First Street between San Carlos and San Salvador Streets in 1892. Behind him are, from left to right, officer Jim Monahan, Mike Burkin, Captain Scott, James Prindiville, and A.E. McClintock. Parades were quite frequent in the downtown area and were cause for great excitement and community involvement. San Jose police officers took great pride in being a part of the celebration, and almost the entire department participated in these events.

Officer Manuel Castillo (1848–1927), badge No. 11, was born in Mexico and traveled to Northern California with his family in the 1850s, becoming an American citizen in 1869. Castillo started his law enforcement career as a Santa Clara County sheriff's deputy assigned to the New Almaden township. He was hired by San Jose Police on December 17, 1896, at the age of 48 and resigned 12 years later on August 31, 1908. According to his family, he stepped down to allow younger officers to do the job. (Courtesy of the Amaral-Lombard family.)

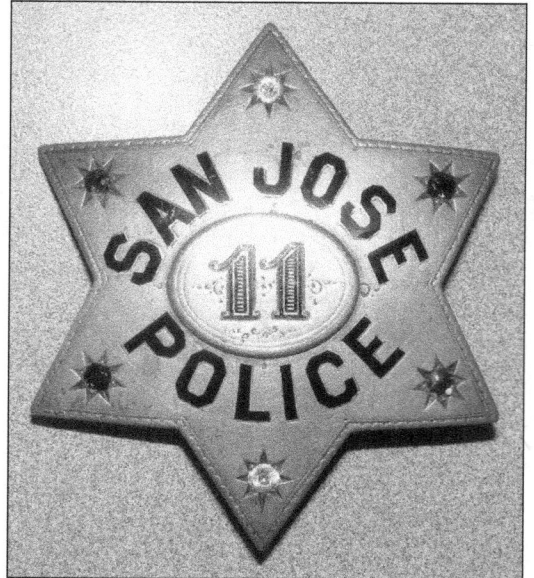

Officer Manuel Castillo is pictured at his assigned post some time around the turn of the century. This photograph was taken just outside of the post office on Market Street (now the San Jose Art Museum). A majority of the officers were assigned to walking posts at various positions in the downtown area. Officers were mandated to walk their posts, being both visible and vigilant. Officers commonly handled everything from vagrancy to illegal gambling. Officer Manuel Castillo's handmade presentation badge (a badge not issued but given to an officer as a memento) was given to him at the end of his career. (Both, courtesy of the Amaral-Lombard family.)

Two

THE GREAT QUAKE TO THE GREAT DEPRESSION
1900s–1930s

In 1900, the San Jose Police had a chief, two day captains, three night captains, and 10 officers. With the turn of the century, San Jose began to grow in both size and population. Traffic violations were on the rise, with horseless carriages speeding through the main streets of town. The favorite racing spot was the corner of Santa Clara and First Streets. Since there were officers posted at every bank corner and in most of the downtown area, traffic enforcement was possible.

On April 18, 1906, California had one of its first disasters—an earthquake that completely destroyed the city of San Francisco and damaged much of downtown San Jose. The "Great Quake," as it came to be known, led to chaos and devastation. Soon after the city recovered, citizens realized that more equipment, especially motorization, was needed for law enforcement officials to perform their duties. By 1910, the department consisted of the chief, two day captains, 17 officers, and two patrol drivers (who at first operated horse-drawn wagons).

San Jose Police suffered the first loss of an officer in the line of duty on July 12, 1924. Det. Sgt. Van Hubbard was killed by an assailant's bullet as he attempted to rescue a hostage. The suspect in turn was shot by patrolman John Murphy and died at the county jail.

During the mid-1920s, a majority of officers were assigned to walking beats. Most officers had to cover approximately three to four miles and check the area at least three times a night. The first police car radio was installed in 1932 and allowed only one-way communication (dispatch could send a call to the radio, but officers could not respond).

In 1933, an event in San Jose captured national attention. On November 9 of that year, Brooke Hart, the 22-year-old heir apparent to the Hart department store empire, was kidnapped and murdered. Two suspects, Thomas H. Thurmond and John "Jack" Holmes, were captured. On November 26, 1933, the suspects were transferred to the main jail, located on Market Street. A mob of between 6,000 and 10,000 people descended upon the jail at 11:00 p.m., and by 11:25 p.m., both men had been taken from the jail and hanged in St. James Park.

San Jose lost its second officer in the line of duty on April 5, 1933. Officer John Buck was shot by a parolee as he and officer Clinton Moon attempted to take the suspect and his accomplice into custody. Buck subsequently died of his wounds on April 27, 1933.

From left to right, officer John Humburg, Chief T.W. Carroll, and David Campbell ride on horseback at the head of a civic parade in downtown San Jose. In the background is the light tower that stood at the intersection of Market and Santa Clara Streets until it collapsed in a storm in 1915. The tower was intended to illuminate downtown and provide a sense of security during the hours of darkness.

In 1903, the San Jose Police Department was led by Chief T.W. Carroll. Other members were, from left to right, (top row) patrol driver D.P. Narvaez, George Fowler, Chris Shannon, Theodore Swanson, and patrol driver John Humburg; (second row) John Guerin, Manuel Castillo, J.P. Condon, and J. Healey; (third row) Det. James P. Prindiville, Captain Campbell, Capt. James Monahan, and Det. George Pickering; (fourth row) L.C. DeCarli, T.N. Hughes, John N. Black, H.G. Pirazzo, and O.H. Pfau; (bottom row) matron L. Frost, P. Mullally, jailer H.E. Walther, Peter Benjamine, and Dr. J. Harris.

This letter was sent to San Jose city attorney Henry French in 1901. Signed by police chief James Kidward and fire chief Henry Ford, it requested permission to produce an illustrated fire and police souvenir guide to support the disabled and sick members of each department. This was the very early beginning of what would later develop into the Widows and Orphans Fund. (Courtesy of the San Jose History Museum.)

This is the first page of the *San Jose Police Department and Fire Department Illustrated*. The guide contained photographs and names for all the members of the San Jose Police and Fire Departments, as well as the police and fire commissioners. Local businesses' advertisements appeared in the guide in return for their financial support.

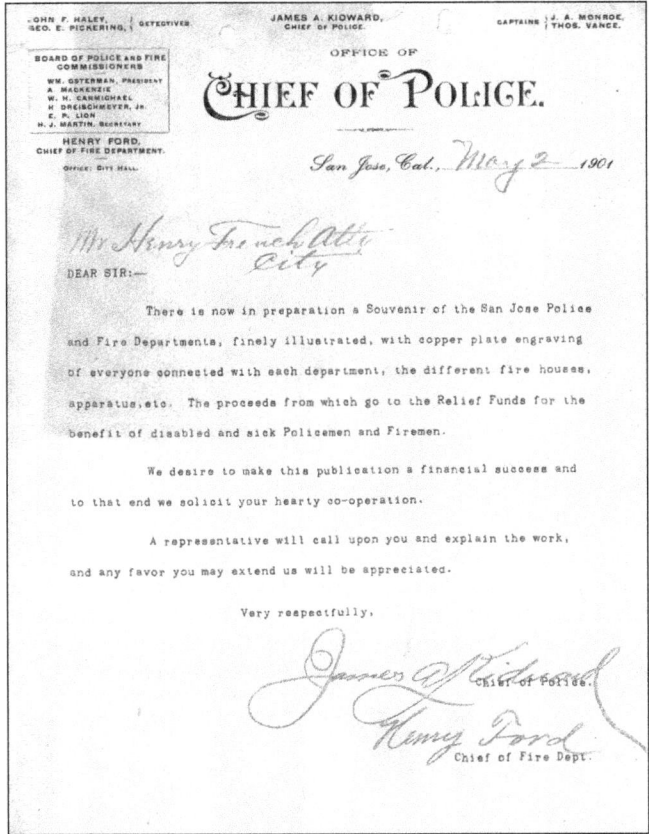

Officer George Pickering, badge No. 14, is pictured on foot patrol along Santa Clara Street in the aftermath of the Great Earthquake of 1906. Although the damage was not as severe and widespread as that in San Francisco, San Jose still had several buildings damaged and some loss of life. (Courtesy of the San Jose History Museum.)

WARNING!

NOTICE IS GIVEN that any person found Pilfering, Stealing, Robbing, or committing any act of Lawless Violence will be summarily

HANGED

Vigilance Committee.

MGIRSON & WRIGHT, PRINT.

During the aftermath of the earthquake, rumors spread from San Francisco that large numbers of looters were headed toward San Jose. A local businessman took it upon himself to form a vigilance committee and printed up a number of signs to be hung around downtown San Jose. The looters never materialized, and both the police and Army units had the matter well in hand, quietly removing the signs as quickly as they went up. (Courtesy of the San Jose History Museum.)

After the 1906 earthquake, a detachment of National Guardsmen was sent to San Jose to help prevent looting and keep the peace. An additional 250 men were deputized by Chief T.W. Carroll, and general order was preserved as there was no widespread theft or chaos. The above photograph shows the guardsmen camped in St. James Park.

San Jose Police Court, located inside city hall, is seen here around 1900. Court proceedings were held by a single judge known as the "police judge." The police judge adjudicated all violations of city ordinances, collected fines, and issued warrants. There were some concerns of possible judicial corruption in this position; numerous cases were reviewed and ruled on by only one person, and the police judge accounted for all fines by himself, which were later distributed to the city's general fund. (Courtesy of the San Jose History Museum.)

On April 20, 1911, the Knights Templar held a parade in downtown San Jose. The parade is led by chief of police George Kidder, who is shown on horseback (center) along with Captain Bailey (also on horseback). The rest of the police department followed behind on foot. Parades were a great way to show off the police force and bring about public support and community involvement.

This is the same parade as photographed from the top of a building along Santa Clara Street. Chief of police George Kidder (on horseback, center) is flanked by Captains Bailey and David Campbell. San Jose was in the beginning stages of industrial growth and development, as can be seen by the combination of cars and horses lined up along the sidewalk and by the trolley tracks running down Santa Clara Street.

Officer Theodore B. Swanson was born in 1867 and was appointed to the San Jose Police Department in 1902. He was witness to many pivotal historical events in San Jose, such as the 1906 earthquake, World War I, and the beginning of the Depression. During his service, Swanson was awarded a gold-tipped badge for bravery for the arrest of an armed-robbery suspect. Officer Swanson left the department in 1929 and died in 1946 at the age of 79.

Officer Swanson is photographed at his post on First and Santa Clara Streets in about 1919. He is operating a traffic semaphore, a primitive form of traffic signal. Motorists had to pay attention to which sign the officer was facing in their direction, or chaos would ensue. Note the slight change in uniform (brimmed hat and short jacket) compared to the uniform worn 17 years earlier.

This photograph was taken in front of the old city hall, which once stood at the center of Plaza Park on Market Street and Park Avenue. It depicts the 20 members of the 1910 San Jose Police Department in full duty uniform. From left to right are James Prindiville, "Dud" Leddy, Ben Kelly, John Murphy, James Murphy, James Monahan, Al Laederich, James Healy, Peter Benjamine, Charles Hertell, John Guerin, Al DeTemple, Chris Shannon, James Salisbury, Ted Swanson, Luis O. Pfau, Louis Sepulveda, Capt. David Campbell, Captain Bailey, and Chief George Kidder.

This infamous photograph shows Chief John N. Black (front passenger seat), officer James Prindiville (driver's seat), officer Luis O. Pfau (rear left), and officer Peter Benjamine (rear right) seated in a 1907 Rambler Sedan on Market Street facing south (note the dome for the Cathedral Basilica of St. Joseph in the background). This is not an image of the first police vehicle used by the department, as was thought for many years, but a staged photograph taken when a dealer brought a brand-new Rambler to city hall. Chief Black and his officers took the opportunity to have their photograph taken, and the rest is history.

In this late-1930s image, officer Herman Schwandt issues a bicycle license outside of the old downtown city hall traffic department. Officers during this period commonly handled all types of city licensing functions, as well as meter collections, citations, and permit issue.

This promotional photograph was printed in the *San Jose Herald* on July 3, 1919, to announce the police ball that evening. Pictured are, from left to right, (top row) Michael Guerin, John J. Murphy, Theodore Chargin, Benjamin Kelly, and O.D. McCliman; (second row) Al Laederich, Edward Stough, Harold Schumacher, Louise Leitch, James A. Murphy, Andrew McCarron, and William Jackson; (third row) Theodore Swanson, Capt. J.G. Hines, Chief John N. Black, Capt. David W. Campbell, and H.V. Hubbard; (fourth row) Ray Starbird, Charles Hertell, John Guerin, and Edward Wolford; (fifth row) James Healy, Lloyd Buffington, H.C. Dennis, Peter Benjamine, and Louis Sepulveda. (Courtesy of the San Jose History Museum.)

In this 1924 photograph of the San Jose Police Department are, from left to right, (first row) Roy Farley, Martin Harris, Patrick Murphy, Capt. J.G. Hines, Chief John Black, O.D. McCliman, J.J. Murphy, and James Healy; (second row) M. Guerin, Frank Raferty, Thomas Short, Herman Schwandt, Lewis Rogge, Ben Kelly, Al Laederich, A.J. McCarron, and Paul Ganshirt; (third row) William Emig, Ed Stough, Tony Russo, matron Louise Leitch, Theodore Swanson, Lloyd Buffington, and Louis Sepulveda; (fourth row) Kenneth Jordan, H.W. "Ray" Starbird, Morris Van Dyck Hubbard, John Guerin, Harold Schumacher, Charles A. Hertell, and Ed Wolford.

Sgt. Morris Van Dyck Hubbard was killed on July 12, 1924, by a hostage-taking gunman in a close-range shoot-out. A memorial plaque now marks the place where he fell at Julian and Fifteenth Streets in San Jose.

San Jose police officers proudly display their patrol cars parked along St. James Park in 1924. From left to right are officers Kenneth Jordan, Ben Kelly, Ed Wolford, and Lewis Rogge (standing with shotgun). Up until the early 1930s, officers used their own personal vehicles for patrol. They were reimbursed by the city for gas and vehicle maintenance. (Courtesy of the San Jose History Museum.)

Officers Clinton Moon and John Buck (driving) are pictured in 1933 working a burglary-suppression car. On April 5, 1933, officer John Buck was the second San Jose Police Department officer to be killed in the line of duty when he succumbed from gunshot wounds he had suffered five weeks earlier while attempting to apprehend armed-robbery suspects in a car.

Officer Ed Stough is seen riding his motorcycle—a 1932 Harley-Davidson equipped with forward-facing red lights and a mechanical siren—and enforcing traffic along the Alameda in the early 1930s. When the officer would conduct a traffic stop, he would turn on his red lights and activate the siren by pulling a lever to engage a gear to the belt motor, spinning the mechanical siren. Electric sirens would not be used until the early 1970s.

A young officer Bill Morss poses with G.G. Good, "making an arrest" in 1928. This photograph was taken in downtown San Jose. The St. Claire Hotel, still used today, stands in the background. Officer Morss is wearing the wreath-style hat badge (semicircular wreath with a number in the center), which was common for police officers during that era. The department changed to the standard shield-with-crossed-batons hat badge in 1933.

Officers Ray Blackmore (holding the mountain lion's head) and Clinton Moon (with shotgun) were forced to shoot this mountain lion at Seventeenth and Santa Clara Streets after it wandered into downtown from the east foothills on July 3, 1933. (Ray Blackmore would later become chief of police in 1947.) Note the white stripe on the officers' pant legs; this trim element is still featured on the uniforms of San Jose officers today.

This is a 1930 photograph of the San Jose Traffic Enforcement Unit. From left to right are officer Earl Rice, officer Edward Tressler, officer William Baird, officer Warren McGrury, Capt. John Pacheco, officer John Sansone, officer Albert S. "Sunny Jim" Margason, officer Robert Byers, and officer Gus Mariotte. Standing above them are county employees Frank Hogan (left) and Jack Dermody (right). Sunny Jim Margason was the first motorcycle traffic officer in San Jose. Traffic officers during this period wore the same uniform as the California Highway Patrol and were considered a separate division within the department.

This is the San Jose Police Department in 1934. Taken in front of city hall, this photograph also includes the motor officers, who are shown with tan uniforms similar to those worn by the

California Highway Patrol. Chief John Newton Brown is pictured in the center of the photograph. He was the second longest-serving chief, serving 28 years from November 1916 to March 1944.

These 1936 police recruits are photographed in front of city hall. Pictured from left to right are (first row) Don De Mers Sr., Jack Wilson, Herbert Miller, Bart Collins, and Stan Ehlert; (second row) Art Philpott, Howard Hornbuckle, and Bill Young.

This photograph taken on October 2, 1935, shows officer Herbert Miller riding his 1934 Harley-Davidson 74 near Market Street in downtown San Jose. Officer Miller's traffic officer uniform is typical of the period: leather riding boots, bow tie, and soft cover (riding hat) with a winged-wheel hat badge. Motor officers did not start wearing helmets until the mid-1950s (they were initially not well received).

The San Jose Traffic Enforcement Unit is pictured at what is now Plaza de César Chávez on May 30, 1938. From left to right are officer Art B. Philpott, officer Edward S. Pracna, officer Herbert Miller, Capt. Edward A. Stough, officer Ed A. Salisbury, officer G.J. Mestressat, and officer A.J. Russo. Officers Ed Pracna and Ed Salisbury were formerly members of the Willow Glen Police Department and joined the San Jose Police when Willow Glen was annexed in 1936.

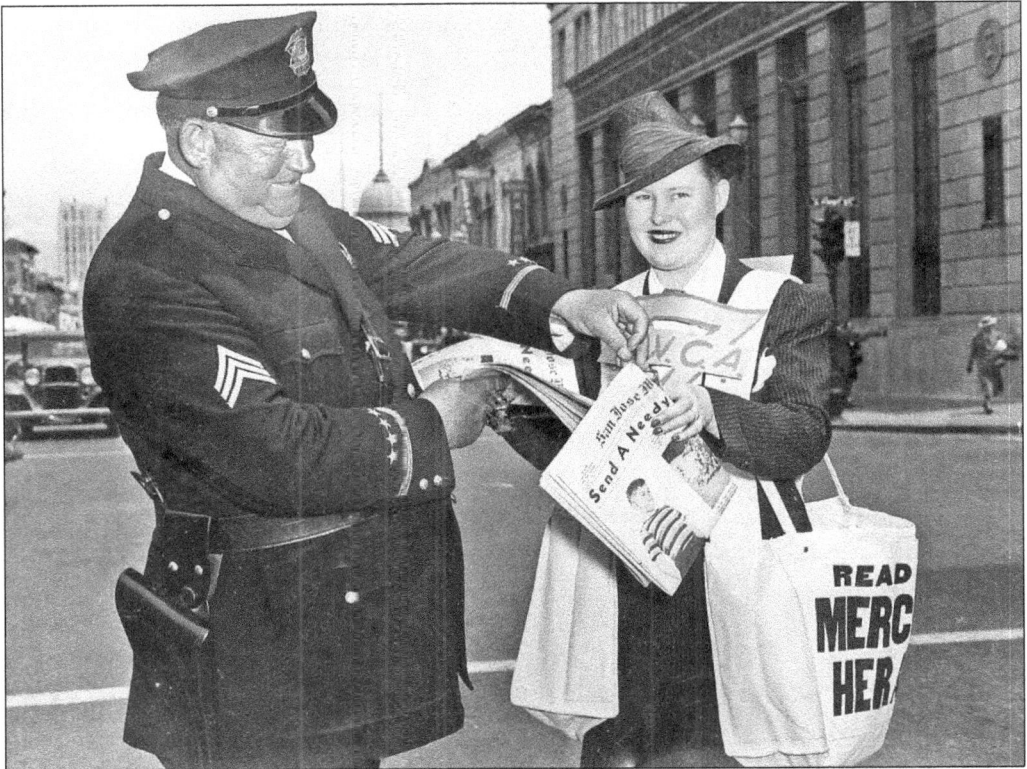

In this late-1930s image, Sgt. Mike J. Guerin buys a morning edition of the *Mercury Herald* at First and Santa Clara Streets in downtown San Jose. Sergeant Guerin joined the department in 1915 and retired in 1942 with 27 years of service. The downtown during this period was a busy hub for shopping and business alike. Officers were assigned regular walking beats and became the "corner cop" that everyone knew.

Willow Glen, California, was its own incorporated city for only nine years (1927–1936) when it was annexed into San Jose. Pictured is the police and volunteer fire department at the firehouse on Lincoln Avenue, which still exists today. The only two police officers pictured (at far right in front) are Ed Pracna and chief of police Paul Smith. Later, Ed Pracna would become the last police chief of Willow Glen. After Willow Glen was annexed on October 21, 1936, Ed Pracna became a member of the San Jose Police Department.

The officers of Willow Glen Police Department never wore patches on their uniforms and had their own badges that were different from those worn by San Jose. Pictured are the two badges issued to San Jose police officer (later captain) Ed Pracna during his time with the Willow Glen Police Department.

32

Willow Glen Officer and Alleged Gunman

...e of the shooting, which took place in front of the attractive home of Mr. and Mrs. Gillum. An artist's of the occurrence shows the traffic officer being shot as he started to mount his motorcycle.—Lomar Engraving Service photos.

In 1931, then Willow Glen traffic officer Ed Pracna was shot while attempting to stop an intoxicated speeder who fled into his house at 52 (now 938) Chabrant Way in Willow Glen. His assailant was later arrested by the Santa Clara County Sheriff's Office and ultimately sentenced to 15 years in prison. The *San Jose Mercury Herald* re-created the event for the front page of the newspaper (Courtesy of the *San Jose Mercury-Herald*.)

J. H. Morton
Ptl.

L. H. Heeren
Ptl.

J. L. Patrick
Ptl.

J. P. Collins
Ptl.

E. D. Anderson
Ptl.

R. J. Blackmore
Serg.

W. L.

K. G. Morss
Ptl.

L. L. Rogge
Ptl.

Thos. Short
Capt.

M. J. Guerin
Det.

E. A. Stough
Capt.

C. A. Hertell
Capt.

L. R. Bu
Ave

SAN JOSE
19   3

R. A. Farley
Det.

P. F. Murphy
Adml.

J. N. Black
Chief

C. A. Murray
Serg.

R. T. Gray
Ptl.

W. P. Mauldin
Ptl.

E. F. Marrs
Serg.

G. A. Carter
Ptl.

K. F. Jordan
Supt. Bureau of Records

Wo C.
Det.

A. P. Philpott
Traffic

L. Green
Ptl.

S. Ehlert
Ptl.

H. L. Collins
Ptl.

S. L. Wakeman
Ptl.

G. U. Mestressat
Traffic

D. O. D
Ptl.

A. G. Kettman
Ptl.

T. A. Fowler
Ptl.

M. A. Horribeck
Ptl.

J. A. Pinkston
Ptl.

D. E. Salisbury
Traffic

E. S. Pracna
Traffic

L. C
Ptl.

34

E. Guptill
Sergt.

H. F. Hornbuckle
Sergt.

H. Kirby
Boma Insp.

J. M. Carter
Sergt.

M⁀Climan
Det.

F. Rafferty
Patl.

R. A. Ganshirt
Patl.

H. A. Edes
Patl.

LICE

Bushnell Studio

H. J. Schwand
Patl.

A. J. Russo
Patl.

H. Adams
Patl.

G. H. Cannell
Patl.

J. P. Covill
Patl.

T. C. Blackwood
Sergt.

E. Wilson
Patl.

H. Miller
Traffic

W. H. Young
Patl.

S. L. Ryan
Patl.

J. Flesner
Patl.

J. W. Jones
Patl.

D. E. Rowe
Patl.

D. R. Kidder
Patl.

This is the San Jose Police Department of 1939. The original photograph still hangs proudly in the hallway of the police administration building.

...RT, a prominent young
...last Thursday, November
9th, 1933. He was last seen at ...a parking lot at Market
and Post Streets, which is a block distant from his store.

AGE	22
HEIGHT	5'11"
WEIGHT	138 pounds stripped
EYES	Bright Blue
HAIR	Light Ash-Brown Blond and Wavy
BUILD	Slender, narrow shoulders and narrow hips
FEET	Flat and he has a felt pad which is held in place by a 2" wide piece of adhesive tape, made necessary by a protruding bone in right foot at the base of the 5th meta-torsal bone.
CLOTHING	Size 10, triple A shoes, pointed toes, wing tip, calf skin, dull bluish-black. Grey suit with a diagonal weave, flecked with a little touch of white, "Brookhart" label in collar of coat, no flaps on pockets, pleated trousers, high waisted. Light grey shirt with narrow stripes and collar points held down by a pin. Grey camels hair top coat, double breasted, full belt, "Brookhart" label on pocket. Grey felt hat with black band and "Brookhart" label in crown and on band. A Santa Clara University ring on left ring finger and a wrist watch.

Kindly use all possible efforts to locate. If found, notify me
by wire at my expense.

J. N. Black,
CHIEF OF POLICE.

In 1933, a crime occurred in San Jose that would capture national attention. On November 9, Brooke Hart, the 22-year-old heir apparent to the Hart department store empire, was kidnapped and held for ransom. The family was advised not to call the police, but before long, the San Jose Police Department was involved. The above letter and photograph of victim Brooke Hart were sent out to all surrounding police departments, advising them to "be on the lookout" for the missing man. (Courtesy of History San Jose.)

CRIME
America's Danger and Disgrace
END IT!

KIDNAPED, MUTILATED, MURDERED

FURY OF THE MOB

WITHOUT PROCESS OF LAW

OUR CIVILIZATION! What Must We Americans Do to Prevent Honor and Decency from Perishing in Our Land!

Before long, two suspects—Thomas H. Thurmond and John "Jack" M. Holmes—were captured and charged with the kidnapping of Brooke Hart. On November 26, 1933, the suspects were transferred to the main jail on Market Street. A mob of between 6,000 and 10,000 gathered at the jail and broke down the jail doors to lynch the two men. By 11:15 p.m., the mob had grown frenzied and began looking for suitable trees in St. James Park to hang the two men. By 11:25 p.m., both men had been hanged in St. James Park. The February 3, 1935, edition of the *San Francisco Examiner* reviewed the crime in detail and provided a timeline of the event. (Courtesy of the California Room, San Jose Public Library.)

Officer Joe Azzerello took this photograph at San Jose State College Police School in 1939. The police school, created in 1930, was the first of its kind in the United States. The program was a two-year training course for young men who wanted to make police service their career. From left to right are (first row) ? Casserly, unidentified, ? Phillips, ? Jacob, Elmer Moore (in sheriff uniform), unidentified, ? Mathson, unidentified, Lou Gerlinger, and ? Smith; (second row) Floyd Kuehnis, Elmer Klein, Tom Scribner, Bob Nagel, ? Todd, Gordon Splaine, Bob Johnson, ? Sergi, and ? Mogenson; (third row) ? Rossler, Ed Jelich, unidentified, ? Judge, ? Davenport, ? Newstetter, Ross Donald, Guy Wathen, and ? Wilbur; (fourth row) two unidentified, ? Muther, ? Tunison, Clarence Johnson, ? Shellheimer, Leo Singer, Loren Gray, and Bill Johnson.

Three

THE WAR YEARS
1940s–1950s

In 1940, the department consisted of a chief of police, two captains, and approximately 100 patrolmen. On December 7, 1941, the United States was plunged into World War II with the surprise attack on Pearl Harbor. On December 8, 1941, Chief Black called for the formation of a civilian emergency police unit to be a part of the police department. With this meeting, the San Jose Auxiliary Police was formed. Out of patriotic pride and duty, men reported to both the police department for service as well as to their local recruiting office.

At the end of World War II, the San Jose Police Department established its first formal police association, the Keith Kelley Club. Keith Kelley served in the Navy during World War II and was the first San Jose police officer killed during the war. The club was primarily a social organization and an extension of the Widows and Orphans Fund. In April 1947, Chief Brown stepped down, and Capt. Ray Blackmore was appointed chief of police, a position he would hold the longer than any other in San Jose before retiring in 1971.

Chief Blackmore's first duty was to reorganize the department. The complaint desk was now a 24-hour operation with an assigned desk sergeant. New, three-way radios were installed in the cars, allowing for both car-to-car and car-to-headquarters communication. In 1948, Chief Blackmore, having recognized the juvenile population's problems that arose from wartime conditions and the frequency with which both parents in a family were working, created baseball teams to be sponsored by the schoolboy patrol program, a predecessor of the current Police Activities League (PAL).

By the mid-1950s, San Jose was growing from a small town into a busy suburban metropolis. San Jose saw a significant rise in juvenile crime, traffic congestion, and even prostitution. Chief Blackmore was a huge proponent of education and wanted the highest-quality training available for all officers (despite having not finishing high school himself). In 1957, a 40-hour training block was created to continue officer education and standards (now known as continuous police training, or CPT).

In 1959, the police and fire communications merged with other city services, forming the communications department. A new communications center was constructed on the corner of Mission and San Pedro Streets to house the state-of-the-art communications equipment.

Officers Don De Mers Sr. (left) and George Cannell pose with their 1941 Chevrolet police vehicle and new camera (with flashbulb), medical kit, accident equipment, and evidence kit. During this time, officers were becoming more specialized and skilled as investigators, thanks in part to the new police school and training provided.

Officer Kenneth Morss poses with his 1942 Chevrolet Special Deluxe police car. The only differences between a patrol car and a civilian vehicle during this period were the spotlights mounted on the window post, the mechanical siren, and the one-way radio installed in the vehicle. Note the radio antenna mounted on the rear fender.

This is a rare photograph of the newly formed (in December 1941) Auxiliary Police Unit during an inspection on Mother's Day in May 1942. The Auxiliary Police Unit was authorized to have a maximum membership of 400 officers and was required to have at least 100 members to retain the status of a permanent auxiliary unit. Members were part of the Civil Defense and Disaster Program, which included air raid wardens during World War II.

Officer Keith Kelley, badge No. 40, joined the San Jose Police Department shortly before World War II. After the war started, he joined the Navy and was serving on a destroyer in the Pacific theater. He died in action in 1944, becoming the first San Jose police officer killed during the war. The Keith Kelley Club was named in his honor and now serves as a benevolent association for department members.

Department members stand at the ready with shotguns and carbine rifles along Market Street in 1943. The patrol cars displayed are 1941 Chevrolet Special Deluxes and 1942 Pontiac Streamliners. This is the same location where Chief Black took his photograph with the 1907 Rambler 36 years prior. Note the modern addition of a neon "Police Dept." sign above the original entrance.

Officers stand in formation wearing full dress uniforms in front of the department in early 1942 (note the absence of the neon "Police Dept." sign above the garage entrance). Sgt. Terry Blackwood (second from left) and Capt. Tom Short (far right) stand at the head of the group, ready for inspection. Hidden behind the officers is a 1941 Chevrolet patrol car.

Officers Glen Neece (left) and Robert Warrick cautiously approach a vehicle with their guns drawn during a staged stop on October 23, 1949. The "bandit" exiting the vehicle is officer Cecil Ayer; officer Thomas Kinney sits in the driver's seat. The patrol car is a 1942 Pontiac Streamliner V-8 equipped with side spotlights and a "growler" mechanical siren. During this period, officers could only receive radio calls, not transmit back to the station. Two-way radios were not standard until after 1947.

Parked on South First Street at Floyd Street, traffic officer Elmer Klein sits proudly on his 1941 Indian motorcycle in May 1942. During this era, San Jose Police used both Indian and Harley-Davidson motorcycles (some still owned by the officers). At the time of this photograph, there was no radio equipment on the bikes, but within a few months, all police motorcycles were equipped with two-way radios.

On January 18, 1945, Officers Kenneth Morss (left) and R.E. Slack escort an unruly prisoner to the holding cell at lower booking. Note Officer Slack's hat and belt, most likely not within uniform regulations. Also note that the prisoner is handcuffed to the front, as was common during that time. The suspect, Charles Edwin Biersdorff, had been arrested for being nude in public—for the 18th time!

From left to right in this photograph from December 29, 1948, motor officers Joe Azzarello, Walt Emory, Ernie Barozzi, and Gil Cardoza pose with their 1948 Harley-Davidson motorcycles, which had just been equipped with three-way radio systems, a first for any police department nationwide. For over 30 years, officers wore uniforms that were similar in style and color to those of the California Highway Patrol, and they were categorized under a separate job classification than regular officers. When Chief Blackmore took charge, he combined the traffic and patrol units together under one division.

Chief Ray Blackmore recognized the need for women in law enforcement and hired the first female officer in 1945. Ida Waalkes joined the department with the new job title of "policewoman." She was assigned directly to the juvenile bureau to handle the growing problem of juvenile delinquency. Women would not have the "police officer" title for another 32 years.

IDA MAY WAALKES
Policewoman

Traffic officers James O'Day (standing, left) and Capt. Melvin Hornbeck (seated, right) review photographs of balloons with Junior Chamber of Commerce representatives Bob Welch (seated, left) and Haley Burke (standing, right). The annual Night Balloon Parade was held on December 7, 1949, at First Street and St. John Street. The San Jose Police Department helped sponsor the event and provided traffic control.

45

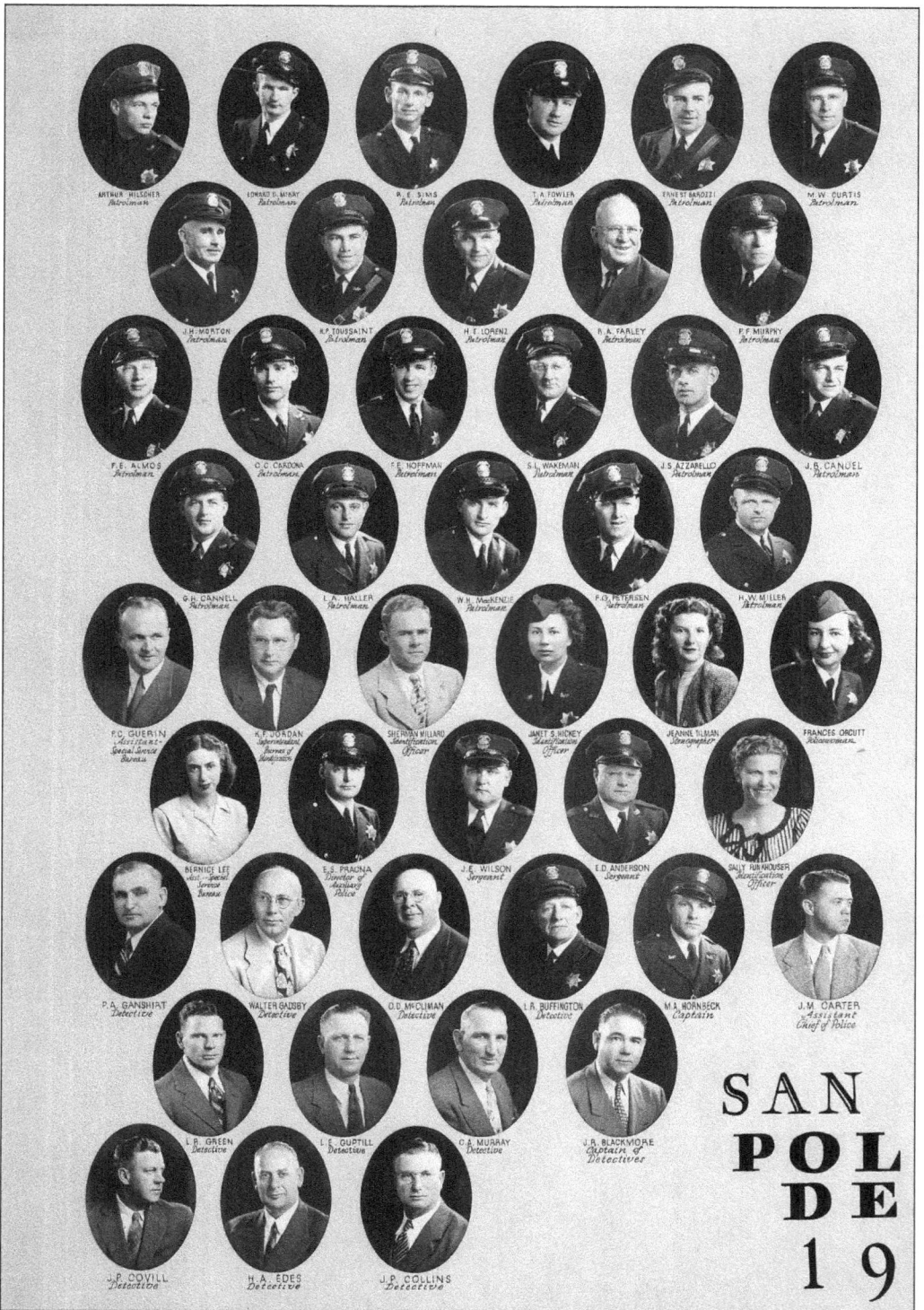

ARTHUR HILSCHER
Patrolman

EDWARD D. MCKAY
Patrolman

R. E. SIMS
Patrolman

T. A. FOWLER
Patrolman

ERNEST BAROZZI
Patrolman

M. W. CURTIS
Patrolman

J. H. MORTON
Patrolman

K. P. TOUSSAINT
Patrolman

H. E. LORENZ
Patrolman

R. A. FARLEY
Patrolman

P. F. MURPHY
Patrolman

F. E. ALMOS
Patrolman

O. C. CARDONA
Patrolman

F. E. HOFFMAN
Patrolman

S. L. WAKEMAN
Patrolman

J. S. AZZARELLO
Patrolman

J. B. CANUEL
Patrolman

G. R. CANNELL
Patrolman

L. A. HALLER
Patrolman

W. H. MacKENZIE
Patrolman

P. G. PETERSEN
Patrolman

H. W. MILLER
Patrolman

F. C. GUERIN
Assistant
Special Service
Bureau

K. F. JORDAN
Superintendent
Bureau of
Identification

SHERMAN MILLARD
Identification
Officer

JANET S. HICKEY
Identification
Officer

JEANNE TILLMAN
Stenographer

FRANCES ORCUTT
Policewoman

BERNICE LEE
Asst. Special
Service
Bureau

E. S. PRAGNA
Director of
Auxiliary
Police

J. E. WILSON
Sergeant

E. D. ANDERSON
Sergeant

SALLY FUNKHOUSER
Identification
Officer

P. A. GANSHIRT
Detective

WALTER GADSBY
Detective

O. D. McCLIMAN
Detective

L. R. BUFFINGTON
Detective

M. A. HORNBECK
Captain

J. M. CARTER
Assistant
Chief of Police

L. R. GREEN
Detective

L. E. GUPTILL
Detective

C. A. MURRAY
Detective

J. R. BLACKMORE
Captain of
Detectives

J. P. COVILL
Detective

H. A. EDES
Detective

J. P. COLLINS
Detective

SAN
POL
DE
1 9

Displayed here are all 92 men and women who served on the San Jose Police Department in 1946.
The chief during this period was William Brown, who served from 1944 to 1947. Also pictured is

46

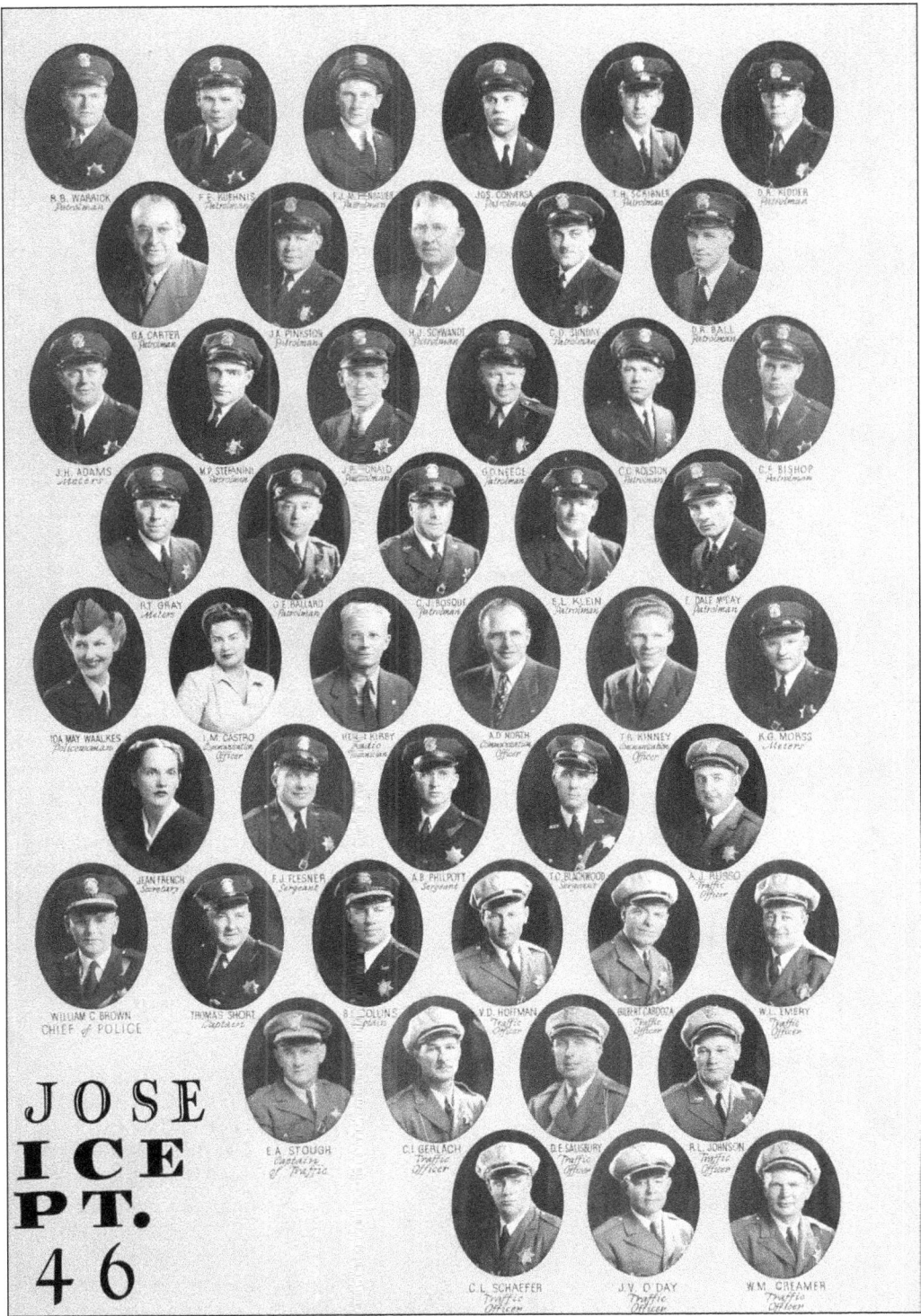

John "Ray" Blackmore, who would later become the department's 27th chief of police. He would hold the position for over 24 years until his retirement in 1971.

The San Jose Police Auxiliary Unit is seen here in 1948. The unit was officially formed on December 9, 1941, two days after the attack at Pearl Harbor, and was made up of men who had great patriotic commitment and wanted to contribute in any way they could. In 1961, the name was changed to the San Jose Police Reserve.

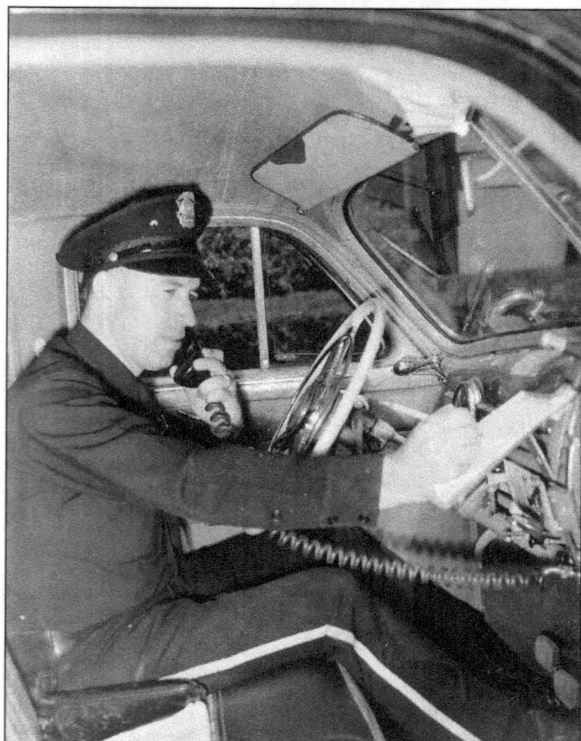

Officer Fred Hoffman takes a radio call from dispatch and writes down notes on his vehicle clipboard. He is driving a 1946 Pontiac Streamliner four-door patrol car. This photograph was taken some time after 1947, which was when Chief Blackmore had new two-way radios installed in the patrol cars (note that the radio hand pack is actually modeled after a phone receiver).

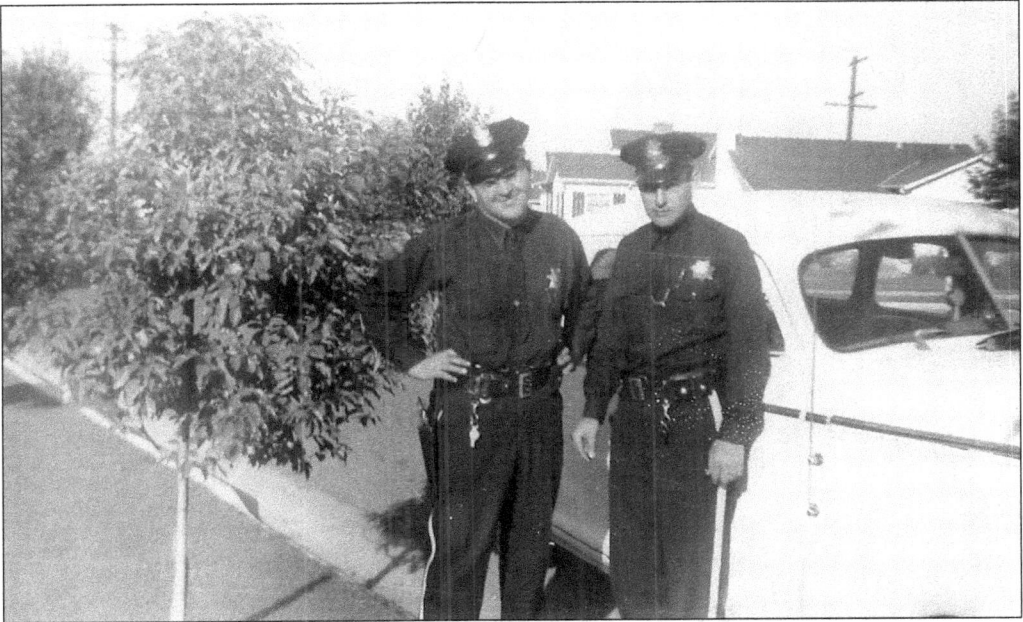

Officers George Cannell (left) and Don De Mers Sr. stand along a residential street in the mid-to late 1940s. During the war years, it was common for officers to ride together for safety. As department resources became stretched thin, more officers were patrolling a solo beat or walking the business district downtown.

San Jose traffic officers pose with their brand-new 1946 Pontiac Streamliner patrol cars. They are, from left to right, officer Charles Cardona, Fred Almos, George Cannell, Joe Azzarello, Sgt. Arthur B. Philpott, and Herbert Miller. These were some of the first patrol cars to be purchased after the war, and they were painted in two tones since they were assigned to handle traffic enforcement.

Officer John J. Covalesk, badge No. 70, served in the US Marine Corps during World War II. He was on Wake Island when it was surrendered to the Japanese, taken prisoner, and forced into the Bataan Death March. He had only been on the department for seven months when he was shot and killed by an armed burglar that he had detected in the process of a business burglary on November 15, 1950.

Officer John J. Covalesk's funeral, held at the Scottish Rite Temple (now San Jose Athletic Club) in downtown San Jose, was attended by over 100 officers, city officials, and the officer's family. After the service, his body was flown home to Lawrence, Massachusetts, for burial. Officer Covalesk's widow (who was due to have their first child) received over $5,000 in donations from the citizens of San Jose, which was the equivalent of two years of police salary.

Sgt. Terry Blackwood poses next to a 1951 Pontiac Chieftain patrol car with its equipment laid out for display. Sergeant Blackwood was the assigned to the police garage and charged with the maintenance and care of the police fleet. This photograph was taken for a newspaper article about the police department.

Lt. Eddie Pracna pins rank on the shoulder of an Auxiliary Police officer in the mid-1950s. Auxiliary officers were assigned ranks within the division that were only recognized within their own rank and file. Although the Auxiliary Police was primarily formed to supplement the police department during the war years, San Jose found that these officers were a great benefit to both the city and the police department alike, providing additional services and relief even after the war had ended.

This 1950 carton artwork was drawn by officer Thomas Short after Officer Conversa had an accidental discharge of his shotgun at police headquarters. This incident occurred just after 4:00 a.m. on November 19, 1950. Cartoons and satirical artwork were and are commonplace in the police culture and bring a sense of relief to otherwise serious and dangerous incidents.

At left is a copy of the original typed supplementary offense report dated November, 19, 1950, from Elmer Klein to Chief Blackmore regarding the accidental discharge. Sergeant Klein attempted to add humor in his report by stating on the last line, "Accidental wounding of personnel at the headquarters would be very tragic, (especially if it happened to me)."

Traffic officer Roy Garringer is pictured in the early 1950s handing out a trophy at the San Jose Speedway. Officer Garringer started his career in 1947 as a traffic officer and later became a police officer when the classification changed. He retired in 1974 as a police sergeant. He is wearing the early traffic officer uniform, which was tan and different from that of patrol officers (note the early-style motorcycle helmet).

These new 1953 Ford Traffic Enforcement vehicles are pictured in front of the San Jose Civic Auditorium (now known as the City National Civic). From left to right are traffic officer A.J. Russo, patrolman John Mattern, traffic captain Mel Hornbeck, and Sgt. Terry Blackwood. Traffic officers wore a uniform similar to the California Highway Patrol. The police department would eventually do away with the "traffic officer" rank and assimilate the traffic officers into what would become the uniformed patrol division.

In 1954, officer Francis Tanner was the San Jose Police Department's first African American officer. He was assigned a walking beat downtown, and one of his duties was to provide crossing assistance for pedestrian safety. Here, he is escorting a couple through the crosswalk at First and Santa Clara Streets. Officer Tanner was well liked and respected by the citizens he served at his downtown post.

Sgt. Ed Pracna conducts training for the Auxiliary Police Unit in the old city hall located off Market Street. Training for these officers was an ongoing process, as they were expected to have the same legal knowledge and abilities as a regular-duty officer. This picture predates 1955, as indicated by the lack of shoulder patches.

As the city of San Jose grew and expanded, city services and departments outgrew their old building. The San Jose Police Patrol and Traffic Divisions were moved from the basement below old city hall in the late 1950s. They took up temporary residency at 273 and 275 Market Street until the new city hall/police station facility was opened in March 1958 off North First and Mission Streets.

Officer Larry Tambellini poses next to a new 1953 Ford Mainline V-8 patrol car. This vehicle was assigned to patrol as it was a solid color and had two forward-facing red lights. Traffic vehicles had white doors and a "spinner" center red light.

In 1955, the San Jose Police Department held its 37th annual Policemen's Ball. Pictured from left to right are Virginia Adams, Hal Toussaint, Chad Ralston, Peggy Donald, and Mayor Fred Watson. Events like this were a great way for the department to raise money to pay officers' life insurance premiums as well as fund the Widows and Orphans Fund. This event and others like it would eventually evolve into the current Police Officer Associations (POA).

This is a late-1950s Policeman's Ball. Chief Blackmore can be seen on stage, standing off to the right. Most all of these events were held at the San Jose Civic Auditorium. Even as San Jose has developed and grown around it, the San Jose Civic Auditorium has remained and is still in use today. For instance, the San Jose Police Department still uses the recently improved and modernized facility for police academy graduation ceremonies.

The police communications room at city hall on Market Street is seen in the early 1940s. Police bureau superintendent Kenneth Jordan communicates radio traffic to officers in the field and marks their position by use of a magnetic board with the car number attached. At this time, officers could only receive radio transmissions and could not communicate back to the dispatcher. The police communications room was located on the west side of Market Street, just next to the assistant chief's office.

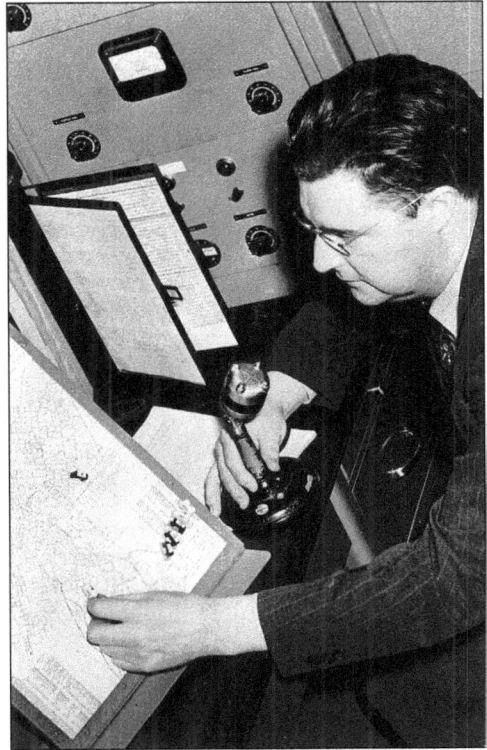

The brand-new San Jose Police Communication Center is pictured here just after it was built in late 1958. Located at the corner of San Pedro and Mission Streets, it was just west of city hall (seen just to the right of center). Today, the San Jose Police Dispatch Center operates 24 hours a day, seven days a week, and is staffed by approximately 130 personnel with 21 call-taker (911) stations and 14 radio/dispatch terminals. The San Jose Police dispatchers serve the more than one million citizens of San Jose and the police with 911 and dispatch operations.

The 1957 Traffic Enforcement Team is pictured here in a city parking lot at San Carlos Street and Almaden Avenue (directly behind the San Jose Civic Auditorium). Posing from left to right are (first row) Stanley Hardman, Richard Erickson, Earnest Boggs, Thomas Kinney, William Campbell, John Percival, William Maddox, Robert Lira, Harold Toussaint, Ray Gray, Loren Spain,

Dwight Salsberry, Walt Emory, Roy Garringer, Mario Steffanini, Lyle Hunt, Robert Harpainter, Donald Edwards, David Adams, James Manthey, Rolland Miller, and Lloyd Warthan; (second row) assistant chief of police George Cannell, Lt. Dale McCay, Capt. Melvin Hornbeck, and a local motorcycle mechanic.

The new San Jose Police Records Division is pictured here in the late 1950s. This department was located on the first floor in the new city hall at First and Mission Streets. Pictured are identification officers Bernice Saddler (left) and Peggy Donald. It was not long before the department outgrew this space, so a bond measure was presented and passed for a new stand-alone police building to be constructed just west of city hall. The new Police Administration Building (or PAB) was completed in 1970.

Officers Lloyd Ralston (right), badge No. 76, and Forrest Tittle, badge No. 65, are photographed with a suspect in the early 1950s. Officer Tittle is wearing a motor-type leather jacket, while Officer Ralston has on an "Ike" jacket that was popular in the 1950s and 1960s. Note that the hat badge on their hats also have their badge number and the word "patrolman." This title was no longer used once female officers received full police officer status in 1977.

Officers stand at attention while being inspected by Sgts. Ray Lee (left) and John Willis (right). Standing at attention at the head of the formation is Sgt. Merlin Wheatley. The inspection is being conducted behind the newly erected city hall at Mission Street and First Street in 1959. The police department was located on the first floor on the southeast side of the building.

In 1958, the San Jose Police Department had 187 sworn officers. Chief Blackmore used this visual aid in the annual report to appeal to both the public and the city council for additional officers. Going forward, the chief wanted a minimum of 213 officers. Personnel levels and hiring have always been difficult and remain so to this day.

POLICE PERSONNEL

| PRESENT NUMBER IN SAN JOSE POLICE DEPT. | MINIMUM NUMBER NEEDED | TOTAL POLICE IN CITIES OUR SIZE |

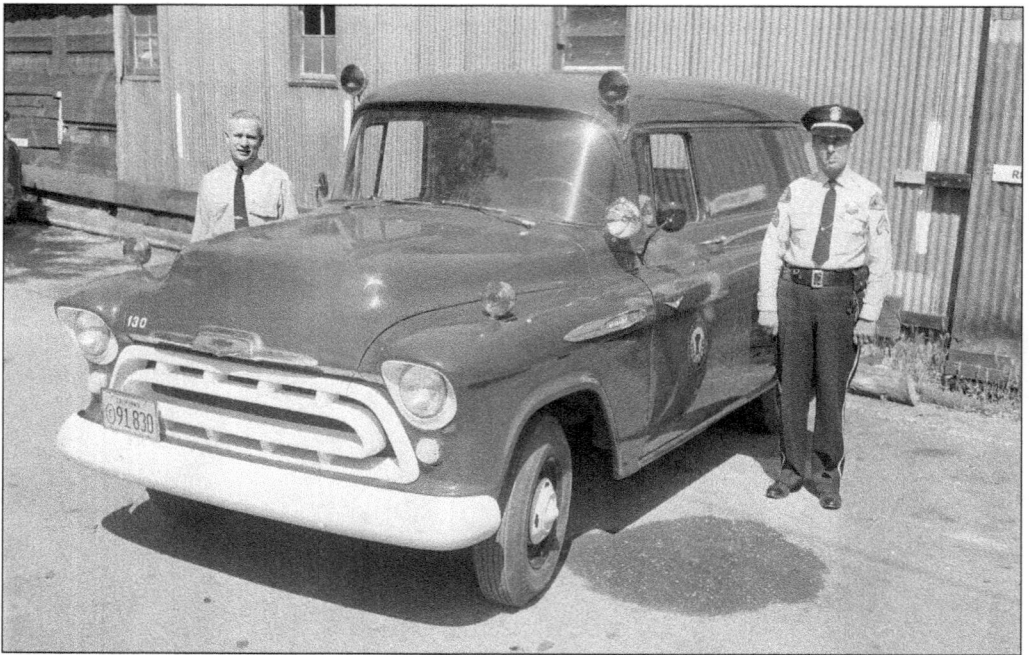

Garage sergeant Terry Blackwood (right) and dispatcher Henry Kirby (left) pose with a 1956 Chevrolet panel van assigned to the Department of Communications.

Officer Donald Edwards poses with a 1957 Chevrolet 150 four-door vehicle. This car was assigned to the traffic unit and was painted with white doors and a center siren. Vehicles 10, 11, 36, and 37 were assigned to traffic duties that included investigating accidents involving injury or death, as well as hit and runs.

Pictured on Range Day 1956 are, from left to right, Wilbur Givin, Hans Gertz, Merle Johns, and range master Herman Lorenz. Officers were taught to be proficient in the use of their firearm and learned different styles and techniques. Here, Lorenz is demonstrating the one-handed shooting position.

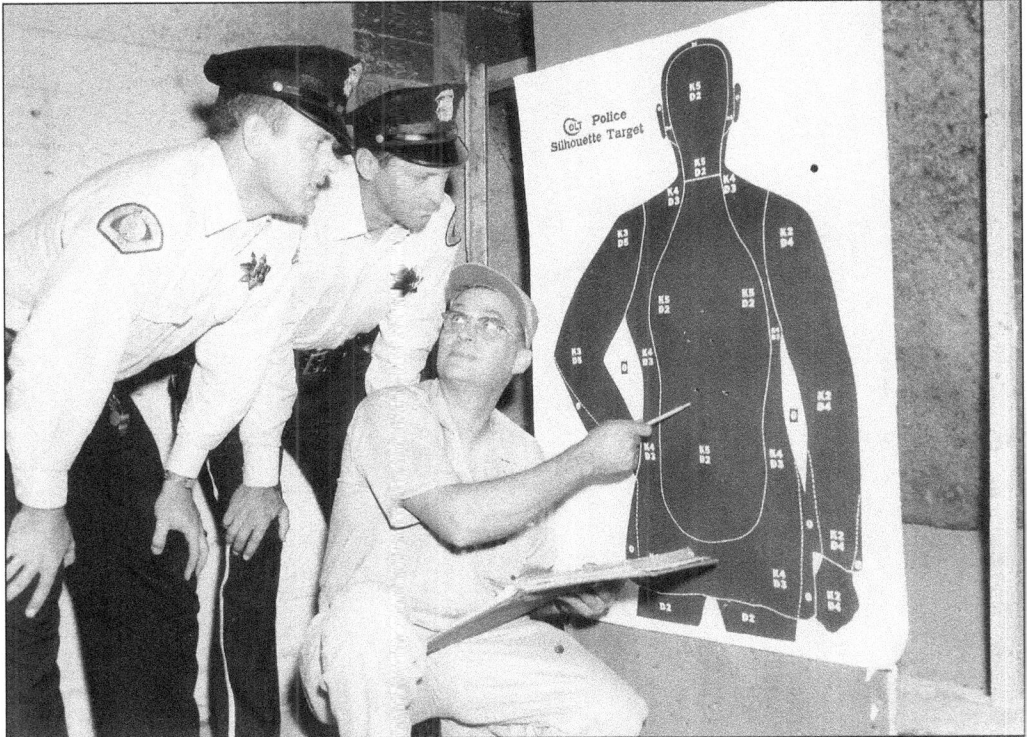

The police range was located inside the old armory in downtown San Jose, just north of Santa Clara Street. Pictured from left to right are Wilbur Givin, Hans Gertz, and range master Herman Lorenz. Lorenz is displaying the Colt police silhouette target that was designed to train officers to become more proficient with their firearms.

The San Jose Police patrol division below city hall is pictured around 1957. From left to right are motor sergeant Hal Chapman, Iona Rossi, and Capt. George Cannell. When officers made an arrest, their first stop was booking, just past the desk sergeant on the right. At this time, the City of San Jose had already begun the move from the old city hall to the new one located on First and Mission Streets. The police department would soon follow.

San Jose City Hall is seen here in the 1950s. City hall had outgrown its usefulness shortly after its construction in 1887. As the city quickly grew around it, plans were drawn up for a new, much larger facility just outside of downtown at First Street and Mission Street. The old city hall was torn down in 1958 and replaced with a new park (now known as Plaza de César Chávez).

Officer John Buck stands by as officer Roscoe Fannucci places a towel over a very slippery suspect some time in the mid- to late 1950s. As the story goes, the suspect fled through a trolley yard as he attempted to get away from pursuing officers. He found a barrel of waste oil and climbed inside to hide, but he was quickly discovered with just the top of his head sticking out of the barrel. He was unceremoniously escorted to jail in the back of a police wagon, minus his oily clothes.

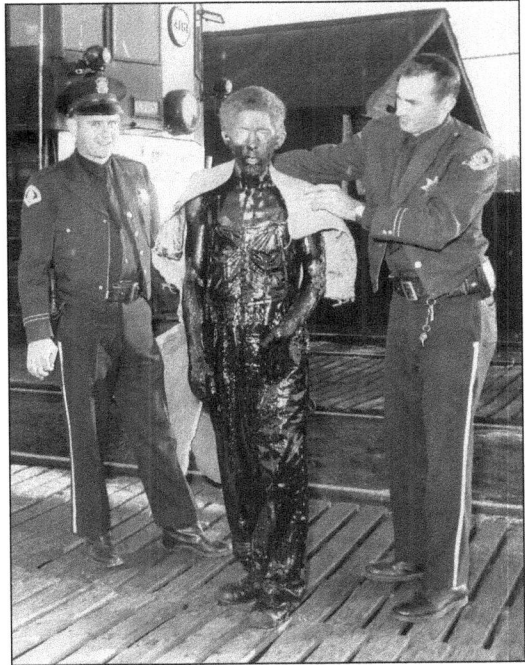

The San Jose Police Department patrol division is pictured in 1958. This photograph was taken in an empty parking lot behind the San Jose Civic Auditorium along San Carlos Street and Almaden Boulevard. Along with the 1950s Harley-Davidson motorcycles are 1957 Chevrolets and 1957–1958 Fords.

This is the booking area in old city hall along Market Street in May 1957. From left to right are Bud Bosque, Don Kidder, an unidentified arrestee, and Herman Lorenz. Officers would book their prisoners in the holding cells in the basement. After the police department moved from downtown, prisoners were booked into the county jail located on San Pedro Street at Hedding Street.

Officer Steve Chesley starts his patrol shift in a 1957 Ford patrol car along Mission Street in the late 1950s. The Ford is equipped with the latest Motorola radio equipment with two separate radio channels and three-way broadcasting. San Jose had two radio channels: blue and green. Officers would toggle a switch to go between the two, depending on which part of the city they were working in.

Four

A DECADE OF PROTEST AND TURBULENCE
1960s

The 1960s brought much social change to America, and the San Jose Police Department was no exception. Officers in 1960 were still performing their duties in the downtown as they had for over 80 years, which meant foot patrol on a 24-hour basis. Because of annexation and sprawl, officers were then patrolling over 74 square miles of city, most of it still rural and farmland. Story and King Roads intersected with a four-way stop sign, with Prusch Farm on one corner and a milking barn on the other. A Hancock gas station on the southeast corner was the only indication of commercial development.

San Jose State University had what was considered the first incident of college unrest. On November 21, 1967, a student protest against the Vietnam War and Dow Chemical Company resulted in a large riot during which tear gas was deployed and numerous people suffered injuries. As the war escalated, so did student protests across the nation. The San Jose Riot Squad was formed in 1969 and not only handled San Jose protests but also responded to assist Berkeley police with several protests there.

The combination of a growing population and times of unrest brought a rise in crime. Chief Blackmore recognized that a special unit would be needed to deal with crime in a new way. He designated Capt. Bill Brown to form a specialized unit with high-quality officers to proactively arrest law violators. This unit became known as the "H-Cars" (later, this concept developed into a special operations unit called MERGE).

San Jose continued its growth, annexing the small town of Alviso in 1968. More special units were created in the 1960s, including the Police Athletic League Cadets, Canine Corps (later K-9), and crowd control (later Rapid Deployment Team).

The community attitude toward the police changed in the late 1960s. People began to openly question authority. Officers exchanged their soft hats for helmets as safety became more paramount than uniformity. San Jose officers began to be confronted with a new challenge—police work that consisted not only of community service but also of handling a new type of violence.

Patrolman Harold Spangenberg, badge No. 145, surveys a trash can at 1345 Milton Way, where a newborn infant was found abandoned on Thursday, January 4, 1962. (The baby survived the incident.)

Prior to police cars being specially built for the purpose, extra police equipment had to be added. The Stewart Warner speedometer mounted on the dashboard was used by officers to "lock in" the violator's speed before pulling them over. The officer could then walk the driver back to his vehicle and show him or her the speed at which he or she had been clocked.

This is the first San Jose Police Department Canine Corps in 1960. All of the dogs were donated to the officers. From left to right are Don Moore with Flint, Bill Anderson with Shadow, Bill Bailey with Stormy, and Ralph Macke with Frita. Sgt. John Collins was the unit's first supervisor.

Deputy chief Elmer Klein (standing, left), Capt. Edward Pracna (standing, right) and Chief Ray Blackmore (seated) review a map of San Jose on October 10, 1961. The photograph shows the redrawn districts and numbered "beat" system changes to provide better police service to the growing city.

San Jose Police dispatchers Ron Morrell (left) and George Burton dispatch calls for service from the new and updated communications center at San Pedro Street and Mission Street. Both men handled citizen calls and police dispatch duties, tasks that are now broken up between call-takers, dispatchers, and dispatch supervisors.

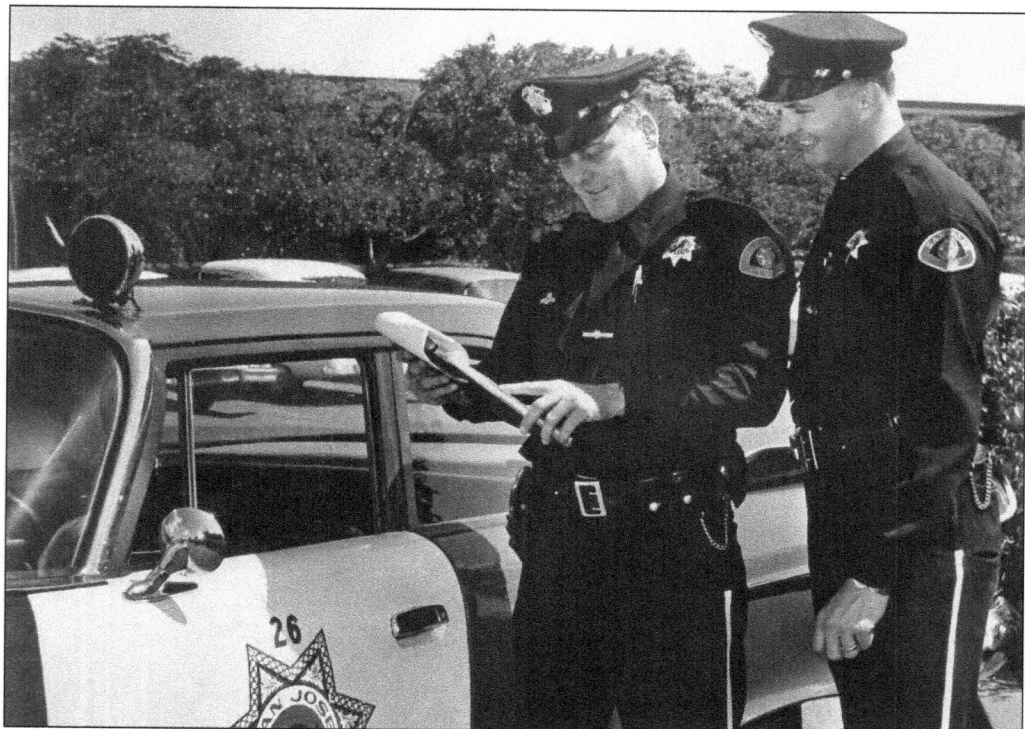

Officers Bruce Moore (left) and Vic Eastman review a report next to their 1961 Plymouth Savoy in June 1964. Both the uniform patch and police door symbol have remained largely unchanged and are still in use today.

Here is the San Jose Police Department, located at the corner of First and Mission Streets in San Jose. The police department was housed in the east corner of city hall from 1958 to 1969. The department quickly outgrew that location, so a bond measure was passed for a new stand-alone building, which was completed in 1970 at 201 West Mission Street, just west of city hall, and is still in use today.

Patrol officers attend briefing on the first floor of the police department prior to going out on patrol. Police officers are, from left to right, Floyd Marshall, Steve Chesley, Art Hilsher, Bob Moir, Lt. Ed Pracna (standing), Dick Thomas, Sgt. Stan Hardmen (behind podium), two unidentified, William Poelle, and Dick Hill.

San Jose Police H-Units are pictured in the rear of city hall in 1963. The H-Cars, as they came to be known, were the first special-operations units in the department. These officers were hand selected and assigned as two-man units to make felony arrests. From left to right (and front to back) are Sgt. Howard Donald, Bob Moir, Glenn Terry, Bobby Burroughs, Joe Escobar, Jim Smith, Larry Stuefloten, Norv Pulliam, unidentified, Bill Wittmann, Ike Hernandez, Ron Utz, Buck Ballard (plainclothes), and Dick Erickson.

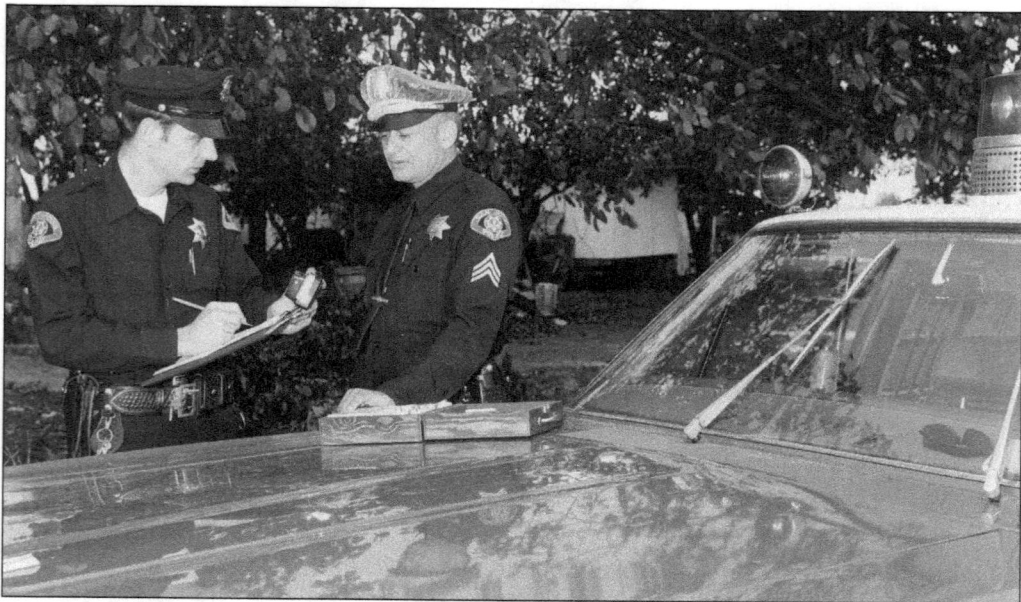

A young rookie officer and Sgt. Ray Lee (right) conduct a traffic-accident investigation on a rainy day along Monterey Highway in South San Jose. The vehicle is a 1968 Plymouth Belvedere equipped with a High Performance 383 V-8 motor. The center police light was mounted higher on the cars assigned to Monterey Highway to add visibility for motorists. Monterey Highway was the main route from San Francisco to Los Angeles before Highway 101 was completed. It was nicknamed "Blood Alley" because of the high number of traffic accidents.

Officer Dick Hunter (standing) gives a tour of the police department to a group of middle school children. Here, he is pointing out different equipment on the police Harley-Davidson Electra Glide motorcycle. Seated on the motorcycle is Bob Kosavilka. Officer Hunter is also wearing a helmet, which became standard practice for patrol during the civil unrest of the 1960s.

Officer Ken Lanch (center, facing camera) and other Santa Clara County detectives display a collection of recovered stolen items after a recent arrest. The San Jose Police Department created the Burglary Prevention Unit (also known as BPU) in the mid-1960s to deal with the growing problem of burglary and theft. The San Jose Police Department has always found innovative ways to deal with different crime trends and formed specialized units and task forces within the department to address them.

Det. Jim Barnett is shown making an arrest of a suspect somewhere in the downtown area. He is carrying a standard police-issue six-shot Smith & Wesson Model 58 revolver. The San Jose Police Department would not issue semiautomatic firearms until the late 1980s.

Officer Richard Cadenasso stands next to a new 1968 Plymouth Belvedere patrol car. This vehicle was equipped with a 383 police interceptor engine. The 1968 Plymouth Belvedere is considered by many to be one of the best police cars to ever come out of Detroit. This photograph was taken in front of the police garage located on San Pedro Street, which is still used by the police department today.

This image from May 1966 shows the members of the newly chartered San Jose Explorers Program being taught proper gun safety by a police reserve. The Explorers Program began with the support of Chief Blackmore and was overseen by officer Gary Rosso. The unit would later change its name to the PAL Law Enforcement Cadets.

The badge and patch was worn by the Explorers in 1966. They were designed to be different from those worn by sworn police officers in order to prevent any confusion of authority by the public.

Officer Larry Darr sits in the driver's seat of his unmarked 1963 Dodge 330 H-Car. He was assigned as H-8 when this photograph was taken in 1966. Officer Darr was a former Marine Corps drill instructor and later became a sergeant in the department. He would be known for his expertise in robbery and would teach other departments statewide.

Identification officer Sharon A. Moore, badge No. 1638, is pictured here in full uniform. From the late 1940s through the 1960s, female officers were classified differently than their male counterparts. They had badges and carried firearms (discretely) but did not go out on patrol. They received less pay and were often relegated to filing paperwork or fingerprinting prisoners. Not until 1977 did female officers receive full police officer status and pay.

This is the 1967 San Jose Police pistol team at the Captain Weber Memorial Pistol Championship in Stockton, California. From left to right are Dalton Rolen, Fred Mullins, Ken Lanch, and Bill Brown. The San Jose Police pistol team first started in the early 1930s and has continued, with department members competing at the Police and Fire Olympics to this day.

Here, Sgt. Herbert Miller teaches a group of school safety patrol traffic crossing guards the proper way to display traffic signs when stopping vehicles at a crosswalk. Sergeant Miller was a former motor officer and was assigned to oversee the school crossing guards. Several middle schools in San Jose where aided by student volunteers conducting crossing-guard duties.

These officers are conducting a field sobriety test some time in the late 1960s. Officers Dexter O'Day (left) and Rhett Retzloff (right) closely observe a suspected drunk driver as he attempts to keep his balance. Note that both officers are wearing their helmets. During this era, it was not uncommon for police officers to have rocks or bottles thrown at them while they were conducting business.

Patrol officer George Ozuna cautiously checks the front of a store during a rainy night in the late 1960s. San Jose police officers routinely responded to calls by themselves and were expected to "go it alone," handling calls without assistance. This style of police work is no longer applied as officers are expected to work as a team to safely handle incidents.

Fourth-watch officers stand by in a parking lot at King Road and William Street in the mid-1960s. Officers would often respond to this area due to unrest from local hooligans. This image dates from before the formation of the Riot Squad, which would later be responsible for crowd-control situations. From left to right are unidentified, Aubrey Parrott (with canine Lasso), Terry Boone, Richard Cadenasso, Paul Elorreaga, Richard Frechette, Ron Tannehill, Gary Kieth, Fred Esparza, and Mike Maehler.

These identification officers are being trained in the handling of latent fingerprints some time in 1968. Seated from left to right are Karen Morris, Margaret Anthony Suka, Lucy Shaw, Greta Lopez Shannon, Pat Oviatt-Potter, Marilyn Musser, Phyllis Trussler, Lee Womack, Liz Michaelson, Sharon Young, Sharon Moore, Joanne Penrod Moore, Mona Bond, and Donna Jewett. After 1977, many of these women would attain full status as police officers and move up through the ranks in the department.

On Tuesday, November 20, 1967, Dow Chemical representatives made an appearance at San Jose State University. Many students and faculty objected to this visit since the company was supporting war efforts in Vietnam. Sgt. Bill Brown assembled a group of officers and recruits from the academy to keep the protest in check. At right, a small detail of officers in white helmets protects the entrance to the administration building at San Fernando and Seventh Streets.

Plainclothes Det. Sgts. Hal Lail (right) and Larry Demkowski (center, with sunglasses), along with uniformed officers, move out of the crowd with an arrestee while reserve officer Dick Reisner records the event on camera to the right. Sgt. Bill Brown is seen moving in from the right with reinforcements. This event gained national attention as it was one of the first college protests to turn violent. It would not be the last.

Officer Carroll Blackstock clears a path for officer Rex Newburn (escorting prisoner) as they walk through a hostile crowd just off of the San Jose State University campus. An unidentified officer and Dave Harrison (wearing helmet) take up the rear. As the protest grew more violent, arrests were made for everything from assault on police officers to vandalism.

Officers Mike Thompson (left) and Ken Hawkes (holding baton) survey the damage to the front door of the school administration building. Although damage was minimal and only a few arrests were made, the political and social ramifications were felt through the entire country.

Fourth-watch and H-Car officers move in a diamond formation with batons at the ready during the third day of the Dow Chemical riots in 1967. Leading the officers is Sgt. Bill Brown, who with Lt. Ed McKay trained officers in the use of their equipment and crowd-control techniques. The vehicle at center is a 1964 Plymouth Savoy, equipped with a 383 police interceptor motor. The San Jose Police Historical Society still has car No. 104 in its collection of vehicles.

This photograph was taken on February 21, 1969, during the University of California Berkeley student protest riots. The San Jose Police Department sent a contingent of Riot Squad officers to assist Berkeley and San Francisco with student protests and demonstrations during the late 1960s and early 1970s. Officer David Byers, badge No. 1335 (left, facing camera) and San Jose and Oakland police officers inspect a US Army Bell 47 helicopter. National Guard troops worked together with law enforcement at major protests.

This poster was drawn by officer Jerry Albericci and signed by all of the original officers assigned to the Riot Squad: Bill Brown, Ray O'Beirne, Bill Mallett, Bud Bye, Jason Canelli, Jerry Albericci, Steve Meltze, Dave Flory, Dan Jenson, Rich Couser, David Byers, Stan Kephart, Richard Tush, Bud Harrington, Jay Martin, Dex O'Day, John E. Trussler, Leonard Myers, Brian Gay, Gary Castlio, Gary Thompson, Don Mills, Jim Hellam, Anthony B. Biskup, Bill Gergurich, Gary Rosso, Robert Corrorsa, and Dave Samsel.

This is the San Jose Police Riot Squad in the mid-1970s. Officers are now properly equipped with military-surplus gas masks, web gear (military equipment belts), face shields, jumpsuits, and riot batons. After working with different agencies through learned experiences, the Riot Squad adapted its uniform to a one-piece jumpsuit with specific crowd-control equipment to handle any riot situation.

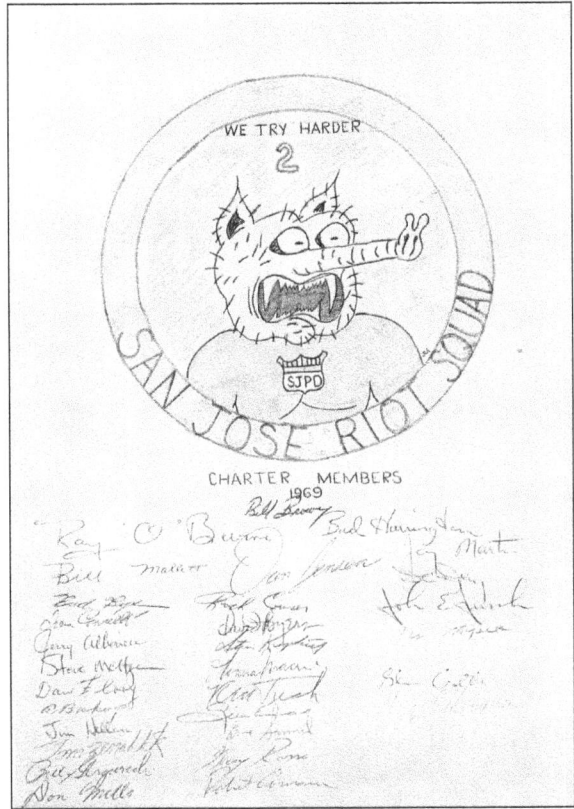

Chief of police Charles Everett is pictured here some time in the 1950s with two young children. He is wearing his Alviso Police uniform, with Alviso Police patches that distinguished him from his San Jose counterparts. Note that his uniform pant leg also has the white stripe like that of San Jose Police. Charles lived in Alviso until his passing in 2011. He was known as the "Alviso Woodcarver" for the wooden totem poles and animals he carved with a chain saw. (Courtesy of the Charles Everett family.)

Alviso, located at the south end of the San Francisco Bay and the northernmost point of San Jose, was an incorporated city from 1852 until 1968, when it was annexed by the city of San Jose. During its colorful past, the Alviso Police Department had a number of different "deputies" (not just police but a wide range of law enforcement and non–law enforcement personnel, including private security and protection) and police officers working the city. The last police chief was Arnold "Pat" Chew, who held the position from 1953 until 1968. Chief Chew is shown in the mid- to late 1950s standing next to his Alviso patrol car. (Courtesy of Kathy Smith.)

Pat Chew is pictured in 1968 at age 64, wearing his new San Jose Police uniform next to the last Alviso Police patrol car. Pat worked with the San Jose Police Department for one year before he retired. According to his family, he was extremely happy to join the San Jose Police Department because he was given a retirement pension after one year that would pay more than what he would have received from Alviso. (Courtesy of Kathy Smith.)

Pictured here are the two different versions of Alviso patches used by the department. The first is a half-rounded shape that was black with gold letters. The second (and last) version was first used in the late 1950s. It was similar in shape to the patches used by the San Jose Police Department and had a sailboat in middle representing the harbor history of Alviso. It remained in use until 1968.

Assistant chief Ross Donald is teaching this group of new officers about basic criminal investigations. This training was prior to a mandatory Police Officer Standards and Training Council (POST) academy. Most training was conducted in-house, and most officers learned while working in the early days. This photograph was taken in the basement of the health building, across the street from the police department.

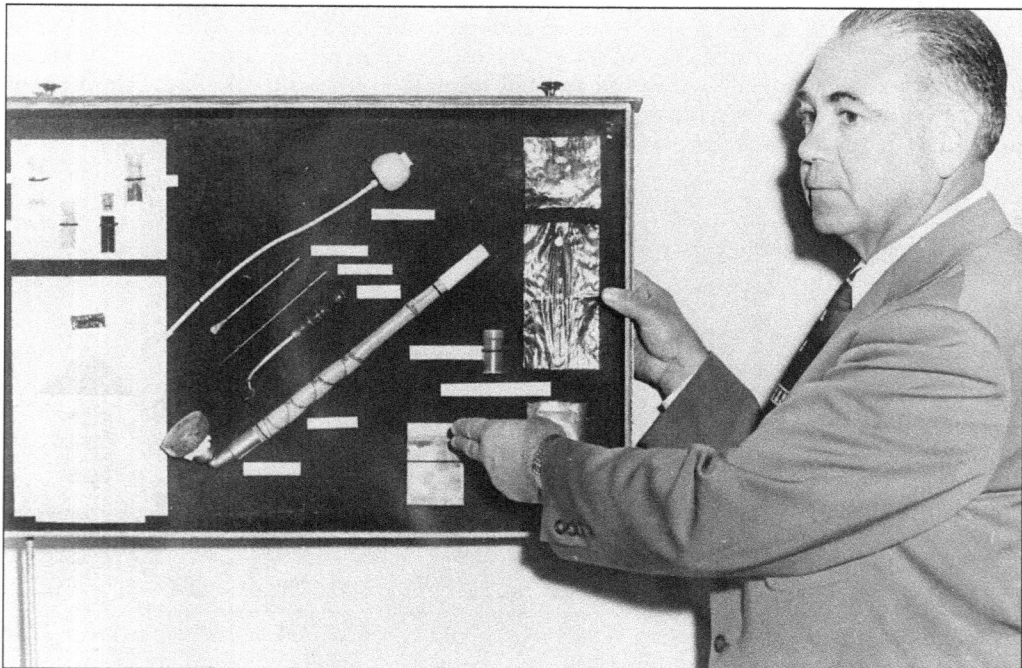

Chief Blackmore is seen conducting a press conference on the dangers of drug use. Here, he is pointing out opium and heroin, which was growing in popularity and was prevalent in San Jose during the 1960s.

This is the police records division in the early 1960s. Pictured are Janet Hickey (left) and Peggy Donald. Janet Hickey served with the San Jose Police Department for 31 years and was the last sworn female to hold the "policewoman" classification. Peggy Donald was married to Asst. Chief Ross Donald and served with the San Jose Police Department for over 25 years. The San Jose Police Department still continues to file and sort records in this system, even after the change to a computerized, "paperless" system.

Shown here is a busy detective and records unit in March 1969. Officer Alvy North (seated, on the phone) picks up a call while officer Pete Deluca (seated, in uniform) goes through paperwork. This was the last year that the police department would be at city hall; a new Police Administration Building (now known as PAB) would be completed in 1970.

Frustrating.
That's what it's like to be a cop today.

We hired that guy to do a job. A job
too rotten for us to do.
Then we isolate him. Fight him.
Ignore him.

That's what it's like to be a cop.
And it's getting worse.

Good men are leaving our police forces.
And other good men aren't joining.

We can't let it happen. We have to care.
Do something.

You've heard it and read it a hundred
times: write your officials. support new
tax measures. back legislation.

Sure, you'll do those things . . . when
you have time.

But here's something you can do
right now, and it won't take
any time at all . . .

smile at the next policeman you see

This advertisement appeared in *Time* magazine in September 1969. The magazine, looking to show advertisers the power of print advertising, hosted a contest. A local advertising firm entered and contacted San Jose Police for assistance. Officer George Ozuna was selected for the photo shoot and spent eight hours posing for photographs near San Fernando and Santa Clara Streets. The advertisement was a huge success and has been reprinted a number of times in different publications.

Five

GROWTH AND
PROFESSIONALISM
1970s–1980s

The 1970s and 1980s brought prominence to the San Jose Police Department as a nationally recognized agency. Through training, education, and high standards, San Jose was on the forefront of law enforcement. However, the department was not without tragedy, losing a fourth officer in the line of duty. Officer Richard Huerta, badge No. 47, was fatally shot while on a traffic stop in downtown San Jose in 1970.

As the department progressed into the 1970s, it reinvented itself with the formation of the Field Training and Evaluation program. This was a revolutionary way to evaluate brand-new officers in the department and quickly became the national standard in police recruit training. This program is still used by many agencies worldwide today.

In 1973, the H-Cars evolved into the new SWAT format developed by the Los Angeles Police Department. This new special-operations team became known as "MERGE" and was tasked to handle high-risk incidents and situations requiring special equipment. MERGE would not have to wait long before it was called into service. In 1975, San Jose had its first hijacking when a career criminal attempted to commandeer a plane at San Jose Airport. Quick actions by the newly formed MERGE team ended the standoff. Lessons learned from this incident led to changes and higher standards for tactics and officer equipment.

In the late 1970s, recognizing the need to recruit minorities and women, San Jose changed its hiring standards. Female identification officers and policewomen fought for and earned the right to be police officers on the same level and pay as their male counterparts. Education standards remained high, but recruits were no longer limited by the old height and weight standards.

In 1981, the Street Crimes Unit was formed to deal specifically with issues in the downtown area, where drug sellers, prostitutes, and thugs had essentially taken over. In addition, the department allied with the South Bay Academy to train San Jose police recruits, forming a San Jose–specific academy.

The 1980s were also a dark period for San Jose Police, with the loss of six officers. In January 1985, officer Robert White was fatally electrocuted while conducting a vehicle accident investigation. In September 1988, officer Robert Wirht was killed in a motorcycle accident. January 20, 1989, became one of the saddest days in the San Jose Police Department when officers Gordon Silva and Gene Simpson were killed during a gun battle with a mentally ill man.

Officer Richard Huerta, badge No. 47, was the fourth officer to lose his life in the line of duty. He was shot and killed as he sat in his patrol car writing a ticket on August 6, 1970. A radicalized San Jose State University student had randomly picked Officer Huerta, intent on assassinating the first police officer he encountered that evening. Thousands of mourners attended Officer Huerta's funeral. In his honor, a plaque was placed in the briefing room in front of his favorite seat. It reads, "This chair is reserved in the memory of Richard Eugene Huerta, Badge 47, killed in the line of duty, August 6, 1970. Brother Huerta will always answer roll call in our hearts."

This is the San Jose Police Department Vice Unit in 1972. The unit, now involved in more than just prostitution and drugs, began to work on gambling and organized criminal groups as well as undercover operations. Pictured here, from left to right, are (first row) Bob Kaisch, Daniel Ortega, Don Mills, Sgt. Luis Hernandez, Lt. Don Trujillo, Joe Nunes, and Bob Camara; (second row) William Sims, Bud Harrington, Jim Hellam, Sgt. Jay Martin, and Tom Frazier.

Chief John Raymond Blackmore served the longest as chief of the San Jose Police Department. He was hired in 1929, when he was 21 years old. He then worked his way to chief of police in 1947 and retired in 1971 after serving 42 years. Chief Blackmore was instrumental in changing the police job in San Jose into a professional career, calling for college as a minimum requirement. He also developed relationships and trust with the community and city leaders alike.

Seen here are the first field training officers (known as FTOs) for the new San Jose Police Department recruit field training program in 1972. This photograph was taken at Pajaro Dunes south of Santa Cruz at a formal training seminar conducted by Oakland Police Department. From left to right are (first row) unidentified, Lew Smith, Mike Miceli, and Glen Kaminsky, (standing) Ron McFall, Mike Nichols, Jim McCrew, Robert Gummow, Joe Nunes, unidentified, Jack Morris, Robert Allen, and Richard Yuhas. The San Jose Police Department FTO program would develop and be used throughout the nation, becoming the standard in recruit field training.

Reserve chief George Cochran (far left) inspects a group of San Jose Police Reserve officers on December 18, 1972. The Reserves, as they had come to be known, had been in existence for 31 years and totaled 117 dedicated part-time officers. Lt. Lawrence Tambellini commanded the group of volunteer officers, who were on call 24 hours a day and were required to attend two training nights a month.

Officer Jim Aligo, badge No. 1451, poses with his K-9 partner, Cooper. Cooper's full name was Cooper Vom Muhlenbruch, and he served with the San Jose Police K-9 Unit from 1974 through 1979. During his career, he had 65 felony finds and 12 recovered guns and weapons, assisted in the recovery of over $15,000 in stolen property, and located a missing two-year-old who had wandered away from home.

The newly created MERGE Unit is seen here in 1973. This is the San Jose Police equivalent of a SWAT team, MERGE being an acronym for Mobile Emergency Response Group and Equipment. Among those pictured are Deputy Chief William MacKenzie (in business suit), Capt. Bill Brown (left of chief), and Lt. Ivan Comelli (right of chief). MERGE consisted of three teams, which were lead by Sgt. Chuck Molosky, Sgt. Ron Rosso, and Sgt. Jim Emmons.

In this 1976 MERGE photograph are, from left to right, (first row) Allen McCulloch, Kent Cossey, Joe Brockman, Brent Pascoe, Dan McTeage, Tim Skalland, Gary Hughes, Dave Witmer, Ray Swanson, Steve Kirkendahl, and Sgt. Mike Van Dyke; (second row) Anton Erickson, Craig Buckhout, Lew Smith, Don Hale, Ron Webster, Gary Olsen, John Strickland, Bob Burchfield, and Dennis Armstrong; (third row) Lt. Ed Melz, Sgt. Mike Maehler, Jack Baxter, Harry Stangel, Carlos Paredes, Tom Cannell, Charles Seaton, Jeff Wilson, Randy Cardin, Ron Habina, Dan Archie, Greg Sekany, and Sgt. Jerry Albericci; (fourth row) Sgt. Doug Wright, Mike Miceli, Ron Mozley, Richard Botar, Terry Moudakas, Joe Nunes, Jim Spence, Jim Baggott, Mike Davis, Steve D'Arcy, and George Sachtleben.

Officer Charles Lintern (left), badge No. 1585, and Jim Carlton, badge No. 1333, stand outside the police garage on San Pedro Street with a Dodge Monaco traffic patrol unit. The odd light bar crane (a "cobra light") was primarily used for traffic accidents, where visibility was most needed. Officers could raise and lower the Deitz 211 police light and also use the side spotlights to illuminate a crash scene. After clearing scenes, officers would sometimes forget to lower the center light, causing problems when they came upon low-clearance obstacles.

Lt. Joe Azzarello (lower left, no hat) stands by with the traffic enforcement unit in the police department parking lot in 1973. The 1972 American Motors Corporation (AMC) Matadors pictured here came equipped with a 5.9-liter V-8 engine and were considered some of the best police cars at the time. These units were assigned to patrol the Monterey Highway, which had a high number of traffic accidents and fatalities. The California Highway Patrol did not patrol Monterey Highway at that time, even though it was the main route from San Francisco to Los Angeles.

This fatal collision occurred on Monterey Highway in the early 1970s. Sgt. Thomas Shigemasa (standing second from right) surveys the crash scene with officer George Holser (far right) and an unidentified officer. Monterey Highway was a rural four-lane roadway running north to south from San Jose through Gilroy. There were no medians and very little lighting, which led to a large number of speed-related head-on collisions over several decades. Monterey Highway is now separated by a cement median, which has significantly reduced fatal collisions along that stretch of roadway.

Assistant policewoman Janie Jensen enters information into a police computer in the early 1970s. She first joined the police department in March 1968 as an identification officer. She was promoted to assistant policewoman in 1971, and in 1973, she was the department's first female recruit to enter the Field Training Program. In October 1977, she was promoted to the rank of sergeant and became the first woman to work as a patrol sergeant. She left the department in 1980 to work in private industry.

On Sunday, September 14, 1975, career criminal Freddie Solomon embarked on a crime spree that ended with the attempted hijacking of a 727 jetliner. After committing several felony crimes all over the city (including rape and kidnapping), the suspect forced his way into the San Jose Airport, entered a 727 jet, got on the ground control frequency in the cockpit, and demanded a pilot, threatening to kill hostages. Officers responded to the airport, and MERGE was notified. MERGE Team 3 arrived at 12:55 p.m. and assumed tactical command of the scene. Sgt. Mike Van Dyck coordinated the team and conducted hostage negotiations. At approximately 1:36 a.m., MERGE officer Charles Seaton, badge No. 1322, ended the standoff with one shot from his Remington Model 700. The suspect died at the scene. (Courtesy of retired officer Terry "Greek" Moudakas, badge No. 1387.)

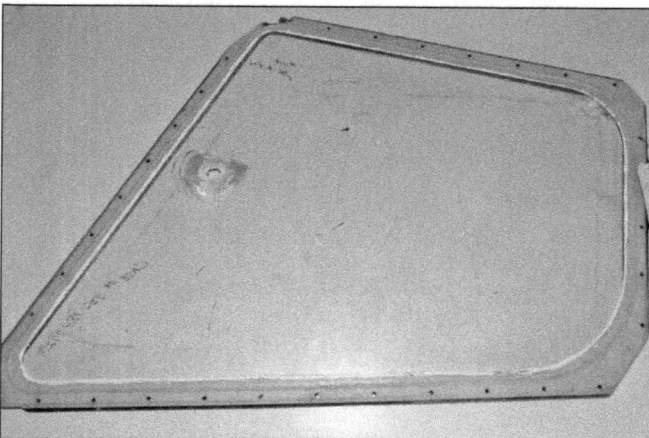

This photograph shows the window removed from Continental Flight 718 as evidence. The bullet, fired by officer Ron Habina, entered the cockpit and struck the hijacker, wounding him. After the evidence was cleared, it was donated to the San Jose Police Historical Society, and it is now part of a display housed at the San Jose Police Department MERGE Office. (Courtesy of retired officer Terry "Greek" Moudakas, badge No. 1387.)

On November 11, 1973, three suspects robbed the Wells Fargo Bank on Alum Rock Avenue. Officers quickly responded to the scene, but not before the suspects took two bank tellers hostage and fled in a teller's vehicle. Officers gave chase, along with plainclothes detectives, FBI agents, and uniformed patrol officers. The vehicle ran off the road at Monterey and Metcalf Roads, where the suspects were surrounded. In the photograph, Sgt. Don Edwards (center, with hat) approaches the vehicle just after Sgt. Joe Escobar (plainclothes officer, center, with revolver) shot the suspect in the rear seat. A *Mercury News* reporter following the pursuit captured these tense moments as they unfolded. When all were in custody, the wounded suspect was transported to San Jose Hospital for treatment. Det. Sgt. Dick Hill was standing by with the suspect (who was not handcuffed on a gurney) when he noticed that he was reaching behind him. He quickly grabbed the suspect's arm and found that he was attempting to retrieve a revolver he had hidden behind his back. All of the suspects were convicted and sentenced to prison.

Five members of the Tactical Team stand with weapons at the ready behind the National Guard Armory on Fourth Street at San Pedro Street in the early 1970s. From left to right are Jerry Albericci, Ray Swanson, Robert Tenbrink, David Witmer, and Gary Olson. These officers received special training and weapons to deal with any high-risk incident occurring in or around San Jose. This team operated in conjunction with the H-Cars until the creation of the MERGE team.

Officer Ann Cooney Moore, badge No. 1639, stands next to a Dodge patrol car in 1977. Officer Moore started her career as an identification officer in 1960 and was the driving force behind changing the classification of female officers to full-status police officers with the same opportunities and pay as their male counterparts. Officer Moore retired from the department in 1980, but during her time there, she was also president of the Women Police Officers Association.

This early-1980s image shows eastside San Jose at King and Story Roads. For many years, this location was the place to go out cruising and socializing. Two marked San Jose patrol units are "10-87" (police code for "meet the officer") with each other, monitoring the traffic. Officers would regularly block off the parking lots to prevent gathering and deter crimes from occurring.

Officer Mike Costa, badge No. 1665, and his K-9 partner, Smokey, conduct a shakedown during a mock vehicle stop on February 18, 1979. Officer Costa and Smokey were part of a demonstration displaying police dog skills at the Santa Clara Valley Kennel Club Obedience Trials at the Santa Clara County Fairgrounds. This was one of the largest dog shows ever held, with more than 3,600 canines represented.

On September 23, 1980, Pres. Jimmy Carter paid a visit to San Jose to meet with Mayor Janet Gray Hayes and other local government dignitaries. His visit was to promote energy conservation and Santa Clara County's important role in that endeavor. A large crowd of more than 3,000 people gathered outside the front door of the San Jose City Hall to catch a glimpse of the president and hear him speak. San Jose MERGE officers conducted dignitary protection along with the Secret Service during the presidential visit. Officer Joe Nunes (lower right) monitors the crowd along with officer Will Battaglia (left, facing camera).

Family members, officers, and community members assemble around Chief Joseph McNamara as he dedicates the new Richard Huerta Park in 1980, the 10th anniversary of Huerta's death. Located on Hillsdale Avenue in South San Jose, the park consists of a lush green lawn and playground equipment, and underneath its sign is a tombstone with Officer Huerta's name and badge number.

These San Jose police officer trainees are pictured in the late 1970s. These recruits started as interns for the department while trying to get hired full-time. They were assigned to the records division as well as the main lobby to handle citizen walk-ins. Some of the recruits in this photograph who went on to become full-time San Jose police officers are Ernest Carter, Don Harris, and Ted Vasquez.

In 1983, the town of Alviso was flooded after levees holding back the San Francisco Bay broke. The San Jose Police Street Crimes Unit was assigned to Alviso, working 12-hour shifts to evacuate residents and prevent looting. Here, San Jose Police sergeant Terry Boone rows the boat, while Lt. Rich Couser attempts to get the engine started. Officers were assigned to the town until all of the water was pumped out.

The bomb squad, or Explosives Control Unit, is pictured here in 1982. The bomb squad was formed in 1962 and was staffed by officers with prior military and ordnance-handling experience. Later, in 1971, officers received professional training after the federal government formed the Hazardous Devices School in Huntsville, Alabama. Officer Joe Stewart represented the San Jose Police Department in the first graduating class. Pictured here from left to right are LeRoy Widman, Richard Confer, Richard Gurley, Larry Weir, and "Snoopy" (the remote-controlled disposal robot).

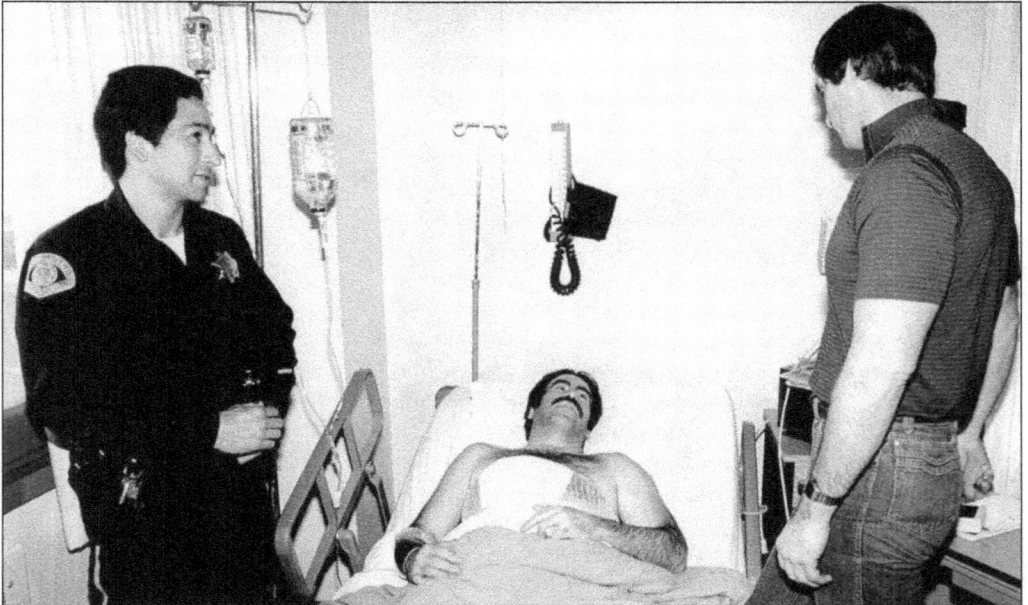

Officer Rocky Bridges (center) is visited by former officer Bill Leavy (right) after surviving an ambush in the back alley near San Pedro and St. James Streets during the early-morning hours of March 22, 1981. Three robbery suspects ambushed Officer Bridges and shot him point-blank with a shotgun. Fortunately, Officer Bridges was wearing a bulletproof vest, which saved his life. Officer Dan Gutierrez (left) was assigned to Officer Bridges as security. By tradition, San Jose police officers always remain with their injured officers when they are admitted to any hospital, taking shifts until the officer goes home.

Mimicking the well-known Norman Rockwell illustration *The Runaway*, officer David Jenkins (left), badge No. 1930, and his father, Arthur Jenkins (behind counter), glance down at a young Ben Jenkins in 1986. David Jenkins would retire as a police sergeant, and two of his sons—Adam, badge No. 3661, and Ben, badge No. 4035—would join the department to carry on a family tradition. The San Jose Police Department has had a long line of family members serving over several generations.

Academy training officer John Carr Sr. (left) inspects a recruit's Smith & Wesson Model 66 revolver at old Camden High School in the mid-1980s. Recruit Jeffrey Kozlowski (left, later badge No. 2520) stands by with his weapon ready to be inspected. The San Jose Police Academy would move several more times until a permanent facility was constructed on the Evergreen College Campus in 1985. In 2001, led by efforts of (now) Sgt. John Carr Sr., San Jose received its own certified academy status from the state Police Officer Standards and Training Council (POST).

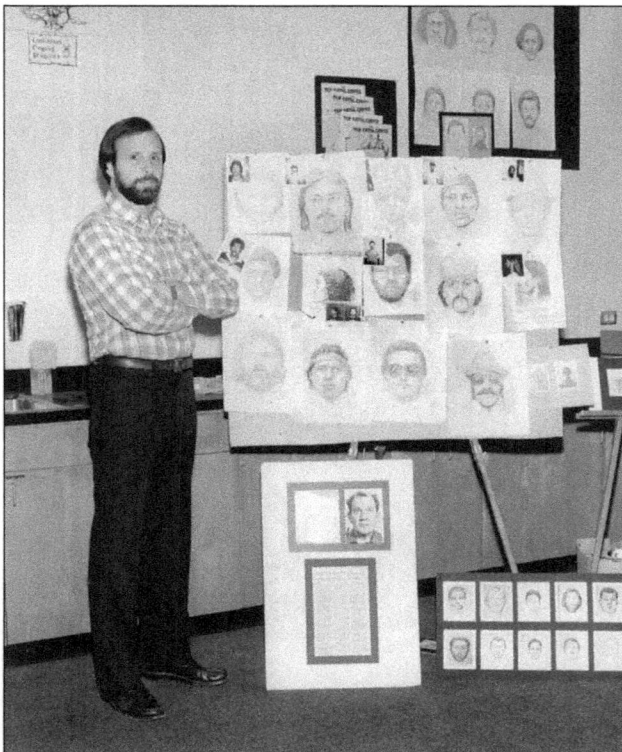

Officer Tom Macris, badge No. 1282, stands by his sketches and artwork in 1982. Officer Macris was originally an art major at San Jose State University and joined the department in 1966. He had used his art skills for several years while assigned to the training unit and was already a well-known artist within the department. In 1976, he became the department's first police artist and was assigned permanently to that specific job classification.

This photograph of a mid-1980s swing shift patrol briefing was taken in the old briefing room under the old Police Administration Building. After the new Police Administration Center was built in 1990, the lower offices and briefing room made way for a state-of-the-art holding facility. It is tradition in the San Jose Police Department that sergeants and those of higher ranks stand around the perimeter of the room while briefing is conducted.

Officer Robert White was the department's fifth officer killed in the line of duty. On January 27, 1985, Officer White was electrocuted while investigating an accident in which a motorist had stuck a high-voltage transformer.

Officer Henry Bunch became the department's sixth officer killed in the line of duty. On July 29, 1985, he was shot and killed by an intoxicated arrestee who wrestled his gun away while in a holding area. The suspect was subsequently shot and killed by Bunch's friend and partner, Rocky Bridges.

Officer Robert Wirht was killed on September 8, 1988, while on a police motorcycle; he was pursuing a speeding motorist when he was stuck by another motorist in traffic. Officer Wirht was an accomplished trainer and also a Marine Corps Reserve officer.

In what was the darkest day of the San Jose Police Department, officers Gene Simpson and Gordon Silva (right) were both killed in the line of duty on January 20, 1989. Officer Simpson had confronted a mentally ill pedestrian who was able to wrestle his gun away and shoot him. Officer Silva was one of the officers who responded to Simpson's call for assistance and was mortally wounded during a gun battle with the suspect.

How to Recognize a "Rookie"

These depictions of "rookies" and "veterans" were drawn by police artist Tom Macris and were commissioned by Bill Mattos to be included in the first San Jose Police yearbook in 1983. Officer Macris not only drew detailed and accurate images of suspects, he was also a talented artist who captured the department in funny captions and cartoons. This particular artwork became very popular and was later reproduced and sold as a fundraiser for the San Jose Police Historical Society.

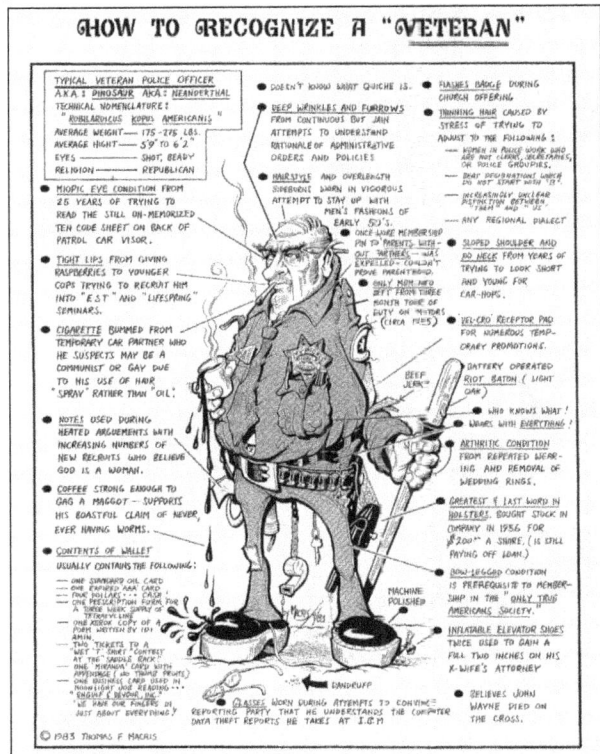

How to Recognize a "Veteran"

Officer Jeff Martin, assigned to the Parks Enforcement Unit, provides directions to some visitors in the late 1980s. San Jose police were assigned to several county parks and would patrol in both four-wheel-drive vehicles and off-road motorcycles. The unit was disbanded in the late 1990s, and enforcement duties were turned over to the city park rangers.

Seen here in the late 1980s, with community volunteers, this community-relations robot—"Officer Mac"—was purchased with funds provided through a sponsorship with San Jose–owned McDonald's restaurants. The high-tech aid was used to help educate school children about safety. Some of his abilities included walking, talking (through a human "partner"), and taking video. (Courtesy of History San Jose.)

Six

ENTERING A NEW
MILLENNIUM
1990s–2013

The 1990s brought an end to an era for San Jose Police Department. Chief Joseph McNamara retired from the department in 1991 and Louis Cobarruviaz was promoted from within the ranks. He quickly recognized the new "community policing" doctrine that other departments had adopted after the Rodney King incident in Los Angeles. The community was again becoming disillusioned with law enforcement, and San Jose police recognized the need to better connect with the people they served. San Jose continued to innovate and modernize, opening a new Police Administration Building along with a new state-of-the-art communications center (known as the "4th floor"). Every police vehicle was equipped with a computer, allowing for automated dispatching and communications.

During the late 1980s and early 1990s, technology began to take hold in the valley. No longer was San Jose an agricultural leader; it was now a high-tech center. With several technology world headquarters located in San Jose and the surrounding area, the region was coined the "Silicon Valley"—a name that has stuck. To adapt to a new and even faster pace of growth, the department began to form different units to deal with specific crimes. Growing gang violence in San Jose led to the formation of a new Violent Crimes Enforcement Team (VCET). Domestic violence became recognized as a serious offense to be investigated and prosecuted, and thus, a new Family Violence Unit ("FVU") was created.

In 2000, the Street Crimes Unit that had dealt with issues such as prostitution was combined with the Narcotics Enforcement Team (NET) to form the new "Metro" Unit. This unit was tasked with dealing with any and all issues that necessitated a specific police response. The High Tech Unit was formed to deal with all crimes related to computers. After almost 70 years of utilizing other training facilities, programs, or in-house training, San Jose formed its own POST–certified police academy in 2001. In 2013, the department invested in community service officers in order to save time for uniformed officers and free up calls for service.

Through its history, San Jose has recognized the need to adapt and change with the community's needs. From the early days of policing to new high-tech law enforcement, San Jose has been and will continue to be a leader in the law enforcement community.

Officer Tim Kuchac stands next to the first official San Jose Police *Air One* helicopter, which entered service on April 24, 1991. This McDonnell Douglas MD500D turbine helicopter was leased by the department for over $500,000 for a period of one year. The funding for the airship came from asset forfeiture money. The City of San Jose paid for the maintenance and staffing.

The Violent Crimes Enforcement Team (VCET) was established to combat the rising violent crimes in San Jose. Pictured here in 1994 are, from left to right, Jason Woodall, Ned Rosenbrook, Dave Honda, Sgt. Ron Helder, Alfonso Rodriguez, Paul Chrisman, and Brian Christian.

The 1996 San Jose Police Vice Unit included, from left to right, (first row) Pete Lovecchio, Phil Beltran, Cindy Kunesh, and Bob Dominguez; (second row) Quan Vu, Kevin Clark, Jan Males, Dave Hober, Rich Benitez, Pete Scanlan, Jeff Marozick, Greg Salas, Garyn Scott, Doug Grant, Maria Ramon, and Gordy Bowen.

Motor officers Bob Reinhardt (left) and Paul Shuman pose with their XR650L dirt bikes at the San Jose Supercross in June 1994. The off-road bikes were a part of the San Jose Police Parks Unit and were not officially assigned to the motors unit. They were used to patrol the back trails and roads not normally accessible to vehicles. These tasks and duties have now been transferred to the San Jose Park Rangers.

This 1998 photograph shows the San Jose Police Special Operations Division. This photograph was taken at PAL Stadium. It contains members of the Motor Unit (left and right) Street Crimes Unit (center, with bicycles), MERGE (left), K-9s, Air Support Unit, Horse Mounted (center), Off-Road Dirt Bikes (left rear), VCET (right rear), and bomb squad (right). The command staff at center includes, from left to right, Lt. Dan Katz, Lt. Dave Hendrix, Capt. Dennis Guzman, Deputy Chief Tom Wheatley, Lt. Rubin Guizar, and Lt. Rick Botar.

The Traffic Enforcement Team is pictured in 1998 next to *Air One* at PAL Stadium. Pictured from left to right are Sgt. Bob Beams, Todd Cleaver, Mark Willis, Jarrod J. Nunes, and Jeff Booth. The property on which PAL Stadium was built was donated to the Police Activities League by Emma Prusch, who provided the land when approached by Chief Ray Blackmore and Sgt. James J. Guido in the late 1960s.

This is a 1999 photograph of San Jose Special Operations. This group includes members of San Jose's bomb squad (left), MERGE (rear), and K-9 Unit (right). In the foreground is the newly upgraded and advanced bomb squad robot, with cameras and more precise gearing for inspecting suspicious packages.

Here, San Jose Police MERGE is conducting gas training in the mid-1990s Fort Ord for the MERGE Academy. New officers had to go through the gas house and take off their masks in order to experience what it was like to be exposed to gas. Those assigned to the MERGE team have always been elite officers who receive special training and constantly practice their tactics to handle any situation that may occur.

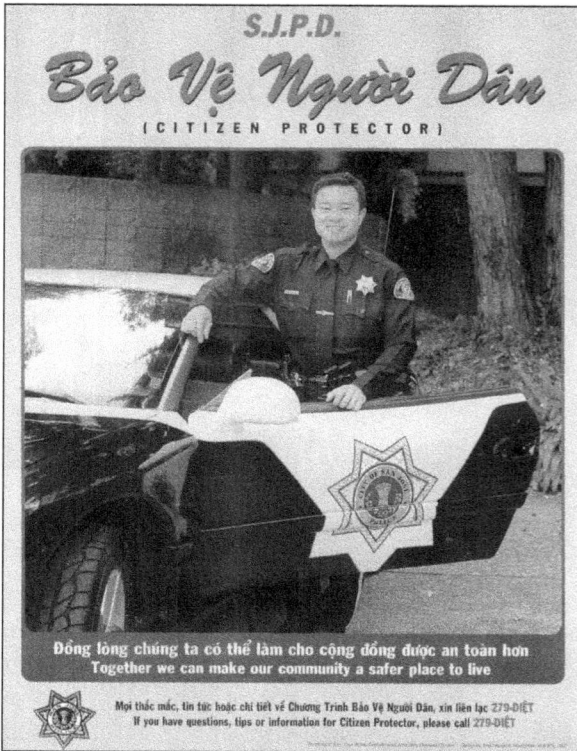

S.J.P.D.

Bảo Vệ Người Dân
[C I T I Z E N   P R O T E C T O R]

Đồng lòng chúng ta có thể làm cho cộng đồng được an toàn hơn
Together we can make our community a safer place to live

Mọi thắc mắc, tin tức hoặc chi tiết về Chương Trình Bảo Vệ Người Dân, xin liên lạc 279-DIỆT
If you have questions, tips or information for Citizen Protector, please call 279-DIET

Officer Khanh Nguyen poses for a community-relations poster distributed among the Vietnamese community in San Jose. As the city of San Jose has grown in size, it has also increased its cultural diversity with hundreds of different ethnic groups now calling the area home. The San Jose Police Department has always found ways to reach out to the community.

The San Jose Police Traffic Enforcement Unit is pictured here in 2011. This photograph was taken at the center of the ice inside of the "Shark Tank" at HP Pavilion in downtown San Jose. The Traffic Enforcement Unit at that time consisted of six motor teams, with five motor officers assigned to each team. San Jose has had a proud tradition with the motor unit spanning over 110 years.

Officer Desmond Casey was killed on October 25, 1999, in an aircraft collision while piloting the department's police helicopter and conducting a flight test in the area of the Alameda and Highway 17. Officer Casey was the 10th officer to die in the line of duty for the San Jose Police Department. He was also a commissioned warrant officer and helicopter pilot for the Air National Guard, stationed at Moffett Field in Sunnyvale.

The San Jose Police Department's new helicopter, *Air Two*, is pictured as it hovers above the parking lot of the San Jose Sharks' arena. This state-of-the-art helicopter has call letters assigned that have a significant meaning. N408DC was chosen to indicate the phone area code (408), and "DC" is in memory of Desmond Casey.

On October 28, 2001, a suspicious motorist shot and killed officer Jeffrey M. Fontana when he initiated a vehicle stop for follow-up criminal investigation. A statue of Officer Fontana, the 11th officer killed in the line of duty, was erected in Fontana Park, next to the playground and dog park. A memorial plaque reads, "This park is dedicated to San Jose Police Officer Jeffrey Fontana 1977–2001. Officer Fontana's watch ended October 28th, when he was shot, while patrolling the quiet streets of Almaden. Although his time serving our community was short, Officer Fontana inspired those who knew him and those who came to know him after his death. . . . This park is dedicated to the life he lived and the life he gave protecting us all. It stands as a living memorial to Officer Fontana and to all those who will continue his watch."

Steven Decinzo is a local political cartoonist who grew up in San Jose and worked for the *Metro Silicon Valley* free weekly newspaper. On occasion, the San Jose Police Department became the focus of his political satire. Here, he lampoons a decision for San Jose to begin enforcement of a new smoking ordinance at St. James Park despite the abundance of more-pressing crimes occurring there. (Courtesy of the *Metro Silicon Valley*.)

The San Jose Police VCET team is pictured in 2010 in front of some local graffiti tags. From left to right are Josh Cote, Carlos Acosta, Jim Lisius, Joe Freitas, Sgt. Mike Dziuba, Tony Vizzusi, Gina Tibaldi, and Mike Ruybal.

This is a 2012 photograph of the San Jose Police Academy. After a long hiatus, the academy was reestablished at the South Bay Regional Public Safety Training Center located at Evergreen College. Class 18 was the first class to graduate when training was started again. The next generation of officers will be carrying on a proud and long tradition.

The San Jose Police Traffic Enforcement Unit is pictured here in 2010. Lt. Chris Monahan (left) and Capt. David Honda (right) stand in front of their motor teams at the new police substation in South San Jose. The City of San Jose has been conducting research into building a substation for over 30 years. A bond measure was passed in the early 2000s, and on February 22, 2008, the ground-breaking ceremony was held. This substation will open a new era for the department and provide a higher level of service to the citizens of San Jose.

Seven

INSIGNIAS AND
TOOLS OF THE TRADE
1900s–2013

The badge of the San Jose Police Department has traditionally been a seven-point star, though some of the early badges were five-point-star and six-point-star badges. Some of the early chiefs' and command-rank badges were specially designed by local jewelers. In the center of the badge was an assigned number that ranged from one to three digits. Badge numbers were not assigned to an individual officer at that time and were reissued as members left the department. This was standard practice until the mid-1970s

In 1976, Chief Joseph McNamara changed the badge to its current design and began using a four-digit numbering system, starting with badge No. 1000 (his own badge number). The numbers were then assigned in ascending numerical order by hire date on the department. Badge numbers were permanently assigned to officers and are now not reissued after the officer's retirement or resignation.

The early San Jose Police Department patches were worn only by traffic officers. There were three versions of this patch: 1) a round, black felt patch with a gold star in the middle and white letters that read "San Jose Police;" 2) a generic black felt patch with a wheel and arrow in the center that read "traffic officer" or "police traffic;" and 3) a round, black felt patch with four red lightning bolts that read "Communications SJPD Officer." Regular patrol division officers did not wear patches until approximately 1955, when the shoulder patch was first used. This design has remained unchanged to this day. The blue-and-gold "San Jose Police" patch has a center seal of a bushel of wheat with grapevines underneath. In the late 1800s, Santa Clara County was yielding the most wheat of any county in the United States, and San Jose was a major agricultural producer of grapes and prunes.

In 1999, the San Jose Police Department celebrated its 150th anniversary. To mark this special occasion, an anniversary badge and patch were designed by Jarrod Nunes and produced by the Sun Badge Company. The badge was designed in the style of a pre-1976 badge, which was smooth in texture, and included a ribbon that displayed the years "1849–1999."

Initially, officers provided their own means of transportation. If an officer owned a horse, he was allowed to use it on patrol. As technology advanced, officers began to use wagons for transporting prisoners and vagrants and motorcycles for conducting traffic patrols. In June 1912, the city purchased its first motorcycle for patrol use.

Not until the 1930s did San Jose purchase new patrol cars, which were equipped with radios, lights, and sirens. San Jose purchased newer and better equipment over the decades as new technology developed, making an officer's vehicle his or her "mobile office" with all of the necessary instruments and tools inside.

These are the patches of the San Jose Police Department. The one in the upper center was black felt and was worn by the traffic officers in the 1930s and 1940s. The two circular patches on either side were worn by traffic officers from the late 1930s through the early 1950s. The San Jose Police patch at the bottom is a first-run patch made in the mid-1950s. This patch was first used by all members of the department in 1955 and is still in use, virtually unchanged.

This image shows supplemental patches of the San Jose Police Department. These patches have all been used on a uniform in a duty capacity, but only by specific units. At center is the 150th-anniversary patch worn on uniforms in 1999. Clockwise from the upper center are the San Jose Police Reserve patch worn from the late 1960s to the early 1970s, a Red Cross patch, the current crossing guard patch that was adopted in the 1960s, a 1970s police officer trainee patch, a 1950s crossing guard patch, two different styles of Horse Mounted Unit patches (worn on Ike jackets during patrol and competitions), and an American Red Cross patch that was worn on the upper portion of the uniform arm in the 1940s and 1950s.

These are San Jose Police cadet and Explorer patches. At the top left is a cadet patch of blue felt, which was used in the late 1950s. The cadet program changed its name to the Explorer Program in May 1966 and used the patch pictured on the top right until 1969, when the program changed its name to the PAL (Police Activities League) Law Enforcement Program, which is still active today. The badge in the center has been in use and unchanged since the 1970s. The patch at center right was used from the late 1980s to the mid-1990s and was replaced by the current style, seen at lower left.

These are patches worn by the Special Operations Units of the San Jose Police Department. Each has been designed by officers assigned to the units to best reflect their mission and tactics.

This collage shows various badges worn throughout the 163-year history of the San Jose Police Department.

These are special unit patches worn on raid jackets and tactical vests by various units. Some are not officially approved to be worn as a duty patch but were created for the members of the specific units.

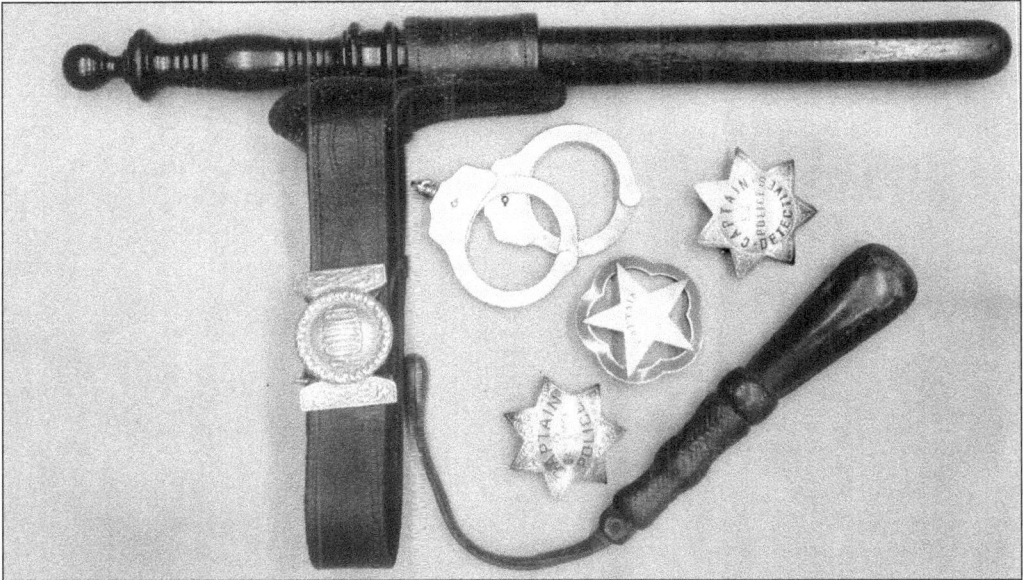

Shown here are three early captain badges. From top to bottom, they are from approximately 1960, the 1910s, and the 1940s. Also pictured here is a leather sap, a small baton that is usually filled with lead or a heavy metal pipe. Its use was discontinued in the mid-1970s, but police duty pants still have a sap pocket sewn into them just below the back pockets. The belt and hand-lathed baton date to around the 1910s. When an officer was appointed in San Jose during that period, his next trip was usually to the local furniture maker, who then custom made the officer's baton out of whatever hardwood was lying around.

This photograph of a 1964 Plymouth Savoy station wagon was taken next to fruit orchards in west San Jose along Saratoga Avenue. These wagons were primarily assigned to the Canine Corps officers, since these officers had partners requiring more room and equipment. The Plymouth was equipped with the 383-horsepower police interceptor motor, which provided more than enough speed and power to answer a call for service quickly.

This brand-new 1976 Dodge Coronet, built to the California Highway Patrol (CHP) specifications, was provided courtesy of Sgt. Bobby Burroughs. He was assigned as the adjutant to the chief of police and, after seeing how poorly San Jose Police package vehicles were equipped and built for service, was able to convince the city to purchase their fleet behind the CHP, at the same quality and standards. This Coronet was identical to the black-and-white CHP cruiser and included the California-only 440-horsepower four-barrel V-8 police interceptor engine. Only 3,852 Coronets were built, with over half going to the CHP that year.

This 1985 Dodge truck was used to patrol the back trails at Alum Rock Park in the east foothills of San Jose. Note that the Federal Twinsonic light bar has been encased in a steel roll bar for protection from low-hanging tree branches or possible rollovers.

In 1984, San Jose purchased two SSP (Special Service Package) Mustang 5.0s to conduct traffic-enforcement duties on the streets of San Jose. These Mustangs were identical to those used by the California Highway Patrol and featured a five-speed stick shift and 210-horsepower four-barrel engine. They were capable of a top speed of 136 miles per hour. Despite the performance and handling abilities, it was determined that there was no need for a police pursuit vehicle on city streets, and no other Mustangs were purchased.

Lt. Ross Donald (left) and officer Bill Campbell pose next to a new 1959 Ford Custom 300. Equipped with the 352 300-horsepower V-8 engine, it had more than enough power and handling to chase down any speeder. Ford recognized the growing need for a specially designed police car and was the first automobile manufacturer to offer a specific "police package" vehicle. This photograph was taken at the newly constructed police garage just west of city hall on San Pedro Street. The San Jose Police Historical Society is currently restoring a police package 1959 Ford to original condition for use in educational and community events.

This photograph from 55 years later, taken in front of the still-in-use police garage, shows Lt. Eduardo Pedreira (badge No. 3104, left) and officer Trevor Condon (badge No. 4262) standing by the newest version of the Ford police patrol package, a 2013 Ford Explorer. Despite being equipped with a smaller 3.7-liter V-6 engine, the Ford Explorer boasts 280 horsepower and handles well for being a sports utility vehicle. This advanced police vehicle provides the equipment storage, performance, handling, and technology necessary to take the San Jose Police Department into the future.

San Jose Police Historical Society president Sgt. John Carr Jr. (right) and historical society board member Sgt. Jarrod J. Nunes (left) proudly pose with almost 100 years of San Jose Police automotive history. From left to right are a 1996 Chevrolet Caprice LT-1, a 1977 Dodge Monaco, a 1959 Ford Custom 300, a 1924 Dodge Brothers truck, a 1964 Plymouth Savoy, and a 1989 Dodge Diplomat, with a 1992 Kawasaki Police 1000 (front left) and a 1980 Kawasaki Police 1000 (front right). All of the vehicles shown here (with the exception of the 1959 Ford and 1924 Dodge Brothers) are actual retired San Jose Police vehicles that have been restored to full service or are in the process of being restored.

Visit us at
arcadiapublishing.com

www.ingramcontent.com/pod-product-compliance
Lightning Source LLC
Chambersburg PA
CBHW050550110426
42813CB00008B/2312

* 9 7 8 1 5 3 1 6 7 5 9 6 7 *